REGENTS RESTORATION DRAMA SERIES

General Editor: John Loftis

THE RECRUITING OFFICER

GEORGE FARQUHAR

The Recruiting Officer

Edited by

MICHAEL SHUGRUE

UNIVERSITY OF NEBRASKA PRESS
LINCOLN AND LONDON

Most recent printing indicated by last digit below:
10   9   8   7   6   5   4   3

Library of Congress Cataloging-in-Publication Data
Farquhar, George, 1677?–1707.
The recruiting officer / George Farquhar;
edited by Michael Shugrue.
P.   cm.
ISBN 0-8032-5357-5 (paper)
I. Shugrue, Michael Francis. II. Title.
[PR3437.R4   1992]
822'.4—dc20   91-43822
CIP

Regents Restoration Drama Series

The Regents Restoration Drama Series, similar in objectives and format to the Regents Renaissance Drama Series, will provide soundly edited texts, in modern spelling, of the more significant English plays of the late seventeenth and early eighteenth centuries. The word "Restoration" is here used ambiguously and must be explained. If to the historian it refers to the period between 1660 and 1685 (or 1688), it has long been used by the student of drama in default of a more precise word to refer to plays belonging to the dramatic tradition established in the 1660's, weakening after 1700, and displaced in the 1730's. It is in this extended sense—imprecise though justified by academic custom—that the word is used in this series, which will include plays first produced between 1660 and 1737. Although these limiting dates are determined by political events, the return of Charles II (and the removal of prohibitions against the operation of theaters) and the passage of Walpole's Stage Licensing Act, they enclose a period of dramatic history having a coherence of its own in the establishment, development, and disintegration of a tradition.

Each text in the series is based on a fresh collation of the seventeenth- and eighteenth-century editions that might be presumed to have authority. The textual notes, which appear above the rule at the bottom of each page, record all substantive departures from the edition used as the copy-text. Variant substantive readings among contemporary editions are listed there as well. Editions later than the eighteenth century are referred to in the textual notes only when an emendation originating in some one of them is received into the text. Variants of accidentals (spelling, punctuation, capitalization) are not recorded in the notes. Contracted forms of characters' names are silently expanded in speech prefixes and stage directions, and, in the case of speech prefixes, are regularized. Additions to the stage directions of the copy-text are enclosed in brackets. Stage directions such as "within" or "aside" are enclosed in parentheses when they occur in the copy-text.

Spelling has been modernized along consciously conservative lines, but within the limits of a modernized text the linguistic quality of the original has been carefully preserved. Punctuation has been brought into accord with modern practices. The objective has been to achieve a balance between the generally light pointing of the old editions, and a system of punctuation which, without overloading the text with exclamation marks, semicolons, and dashes, will make the often loosely flowing verse and prose of the original syntactically intelligible to the modern reader. Dashes are regularly used only to indicate interrupted speeches, or shifts of address within a single speech.

Explanatory notes, chiefly concerned with glossing obsolete words and phrases, are printed below the textual notes at the bottom of each page. References to stage directions in the notes follow the admirable system of the Revels editions, whereby stage directions are keyed, decimally, to the line of the text before or after which they occur. Thus, a note on 0.2 has reference to the second line of the stage direction at the beginning of the scene in question. A note on 115.1 has reference to the first line of the stage direction following line 115 of the text of the relevant scene. Speech prefixes, and any stage directions attached to them, are keyed to the first line of accompanying dialogue.

JOHN LOFTIS

Stanford University

Contents

Regents Restoration Drama Series   v

List of Abbreviations   viii

Introduction   ix

THE RECRUITING OFFICER   1

Appendix A: Variant Passages   126

Appendix B: Chronology   128

Abbreviations

Archer	William Archer. *George Farquhar*. London, 1906.
N & Q	*Notes and Queries*
OED	*Oxford English Dictionary*
Q1	First Quarto, 1706.
Q2	Second Quarto, corrected, 1706.
Q3	Third Quarto, corrected, 1706.
S.D.	stage direction
S.P.	speech prefix
om.	omitted

Introduction

Bernard Lintot purchased the manuscript of *The Recruiting Officer* from George Farquhar on February 12, 1706, for £16. 2s.[1] He published the first quarto of the play on Wednesday, April 12, 1706, four days after the successful first night's performance at Drury Lane.[2] The second quarto, published on Thursday, May 23, 1706 ("This Day is publish'd, the Second Edition of the Recruiting Officer, a Comedy, corrected"),[3] includes such substantive variants as the complete omission of V.i of the first quarto, the omission of Plume's eighteen-line song in II.iii, the substitution of some twenty lines of English dialogue for ten lines of French in IV.i, and the expansion of the dialogue between Plume and Silvia in II.i. The third quarto, which follows the substantive revisions of the second closely, was first advertised on Friday, December 6, 1706,[4] though *The Daily Courant* had promised on November 28 that "On Tuesday next [December 3] will be publish'd, The Third Edition." The fourth quarto probably did not appear until December, 1707, eight months after Farquhar's death on April 29. Like the first three quartos, it includes at the end a list of plays by Farquhar and other dramatists sold by Lintot. Whereas the first three quartos do not include mention of *The Beaux' Stratagem*, first presented in March, 1707, the fourth quarto advertises *The Beaux' Stratagem* and still other plays first presented in November and early December, 1707. The collected edition of Farquhar brought out by Lintot in 1709 follows the substantive revisions of the second quarto.

The copy-text for the present edition of *The Recruiting Officer* is a first quarto edition, now in the Yale University Library, presumably set from the authoritative manuscript sold to Lintot. Collation with other copies of the first edition in the British Museum and in the

[1] "Lintot's Accounts," *Literary Anecdotes of the Eighteenth Century*, ed. John Nichols (London, 1814), VIII, 296.

[2] *The Daily Courant*, April 12, 1706. See Emmett L. Avery, *The London Stage 1660–1800, Part Two: 1700–1729* (Carbondale, Ill., 1960), I, 122–123.

[3] *The Daily Courant*, May 23, 1706.

[4] *The Daily Courant*, December 6, 1706.

Houghton Library of Harvard University reveals virtually no press corrections. Substantive revisions in the second and third quartos which correct obvious errors in pronoun reference and agreement have been included in the text. Other substantive variants in the second and third quartos are included in the textual notes. Since the fourth quarto and the collected edition of the works were published after Farquhar's death and have no claim to authority, variant readings in them are not recorded. Although spelling and punctuation have been modernized elsewhere throughout the text, Farquhar's attempts to reproduce the Shropshire dialect have been preserved as they appear in the copy-text.

The large number of substantive revisions in the second quarto of the play and the relatively minor revisions of the third quarto have not been considered authoritative. At the time the revisions were made, Farquhar was already quite ill; he was harassed with family and financial difficulties; and presumably he had already turned his thoughts to *The Beaux' Stratagem*, which was finished and sold to Lintot by January 27, 1707.[5] More important, an investigation of the revisions themselves suggests that they are not the work of a dramatist revising his play for improved dramatic effect, but of a copy editor consciously regularizing, normalizing, and, indeed, bowdlerizing the first quarto.

The variants fall easily into three categories. First, they represent the haste and carelessness of Lintot's typesetter. A *loin of veal* in Q1 becomes a *line of veal* in Q2, but the error is corrected in Q3. Similarly, *spark* in Q1 is erroneously replaced with *sark* in Q2.

The second kind of variant corrects grammatical errors in Q1, regularizes syntax, and substitutes a standard diction for Farquhar's more colloquial and colorful language. Verbs are brought into the proper sequence of tenses; thus *should endeavor* becomes *should have endeavored*. Phrases like *I'm easily advis'd* are changed to the more elevated *I am easily persuaded*. *Pounds* replaces *pound* throughout the text in such phrases as *twenty thousand pounds*. In more than one hundred instances contractions have been expanded. *Pen'worth* becomes *pennyworth*; *thank'e* becomes *thank you*; *o'th'* becomes *of the*; *d'e* becomes *do you*. The effect of these changes is to destroy Farquhar's attempts at reproducing colloquial speech. Such changes as *haste* for *hast*, *of barley* for *o'barley*, and *make the best of him* for *make the best on him* rob the rustics of the distinctive dialectical speech of Q1. Again and

5 "Lintot's Accounts," VIII, 296.

again Q2 softens the boldness of Farquhar's language in Q1. Worthy's *give a fig for* becomes *value*. Melinda, *the frigate* in Q1, is simply *she* in Q2. The sharp air from the Welsh mountains no longer makes *noses drop*, but only makes *fingers ache*. And pieces of a letter which give Worthy *such a hank upon* Melinda's pride in Q1 give only *a power over* her pride in Q2.

The third kind of variant, which includes the important changes in action and dialogue, removes risqué and profane elements from the play and modifies the portrayal of recruiting officers. The additions to II.i in Q2 are clearly designed to improve the public image of soldiers at a time when England was at war. Silvia is given such additional lines as, "I have often heard that soldiers were sincere," and Plume swears "by the honor of my profession." The deletion of the amusing episode in Q1 (IV.ii) in which Plume grabs Kite from underneath a covered table and causes him to believe for a moment that the devil has really appeared can only indicate an over zealous desire to remove a scene which might be attacked as profane. Plume's sprightly love song (III.i) is omitted as part of the attempt to clean up the play.

Three other omissions of this nature might be mentioned. Balance's remark that "If all officers took the same method of recruiting with this gentleman, they might come in time to be fathers as well as captains of their companies" (III.i), is deleted from Q2, presumably both because it is racy and because it reflects badly on Her Majesty's soldiers. The substitution of English dialogue for Plume's promise in French that he will give the virgin Rose to the disguised Silvia (IV.i) must have been made in an effort to make the play less offensive. The most significant revision in the text is the removal of V.i, which candidly presents Rose's disappointment at not having been seduced by the disguised Silvia. An amusing scene which contributes in a minor way to the development of the plot, it was obviously removed because it was considered indecent.

These excisions did not satisfy Arthur Bedford, who attacked the play at length near the end of 1706 in *The Evil and Danger of Stage Plays*, keying his references to scenes and line numbers of the corrected second edition. He noted that "there was lately published a *Comedy* call'd *The Recruiting Officer*, to render this Employment as odious as possible." In the play Bedford found that "one *Captain* is represented as a notorious Lyar, another as a Drunkard, one intreagues with Women, another is scandalously guilty of *debauching* them." He observed further that "In this *Play* the *Officers* are represented as quarrelsom, but Cowards." He accused Kite of using "most profane Language in Commendation of the Devil." Indeed, "no one who serves his Country," says Bedford, "may escape the *Play-House* Censure."[6]

The revisions in Q2 suggest the attempts of a copy editor to avoid the kind of censure which the play nonetheless received. Clearly the increasing pressure to moralize the stage was felt in London in 1706. Queen Anne's Lord Chamberlain had issued a warning to the Company of Comedians at Drury Lane in January, 1704:

> Whereas Complaint has been made y^t notwithstanding ye severall orders lately made for ye regulation of ye Stage, many of ye Old as well as New Plays are still acted wthout due Care taken to leve out such Expressions as are contrary to Religion & Good Manners. These are therefore to Signify her Majesty's Special Command that you do not Presume to Act, upon the Stage any Play New or Old, containing Profane or Indecent Expressions which may give Offence.[7]

And Charles Killigrew, Master of the Revels, had been warned not to license anything that was lewd or impious.[8] Colley Cibber remarked of these years that "the Master of the Revels, who then, licens'd all Plays, for the Stage, assisted this Reformation, with a more zealous Severity, than ever. He would strike out whole Scenes of a vicious, or immoral Character, tho' it were visibly shewn to be reform'd, or punish'd."[9]

Farquhar's play was apparently revised not for dramatic effect, but to make it less offensive to the reformers. If Jeremy Collier's attacks brought moral reform to the attention of the English public, a growing governmental insistence on a reformed English theater intensified the pressures on players, writers, and publishers to clean up the drama. One doubts that Farquhar helped to dismember his own play. More likely one of Lintot's copy editors, fearing attacks on the play, revised the first edition in such a way that it would be spared some of

6 Arthur Bedford, *The Evil and Danger of Stage Plays* (London, 1706), pp. 150–152.

7 P.R.O., L.C. 5/152. Quoted in Joseph Wood Krutch, *Comedy and Conscience after the Restoration* (New York, 1924), p. 183.

8 Krutch, *Comedy and Conscience*, p. 184.

9 Colley Cibber, *An Apology for the Life of Mr. Colley Cibber, Comedian* (London, 1740), p. 160.

the attacks which might otherwise greet it. However, Arthur Bedford proved that no revision would satisfy the enemies of the stage.

In *The Recruiting Officer* George Farquhar dramatized his own military experiences. When he accepted a commission as Lieutenant of Grenadiers in the spring of 1704 from the Duke of Ormonde, Lord-Lieutenant of Ireland, he might reasonably have expected to be sent abroad to join the troops under the command of the great Duke of Marlborough.[10] Instead, like Captain Plume of his play, he became a recruiting officer. He owed his commission and assignment to recruiting duty to Charles Boyle, Earl of Orrery, who in March, 1704, had been commissioned to form a regiment of foot soldiers. Farquhar, married and with a family to support, badly needed the £54. 15s. he received each year as a lieutenant in Orrery's regiment and was probably encouraged to perform his duties with gusto by the prospect of doubling that income by advancing to captain. Early in 1705, Orrery, still raising troops for his regiment, posted Farquhar to Lichfield. Farquhar's enthusiasm and the presence of captured French soldiers in the town made his task an easy one. In the winter of 1705–1706 he moved on to Shrewsbury to continue recruiting, and from his experiences there drew the characters and materials for *The Recruiting Officer*.

Recruiting in the time of Queen Anne called for more than a pleasant personality and an ability to arouse patriotism and the desire to attain glory. The chicanery and bribery which accompanied most recruiting were well-known facts of eighteenth-century life. In his *Rêveries* (1732), Maurice de Saxe, the famous eighteenth-century French general, condemned "the raising of troops by fraud" as an "odious practice" and described how "money is slipped secretly into a man's pocket and then he is told that he is a soldier." He complained further that many times "citizens and inhabitants of a country can only save themselves by resorting to bribery."[11] Farquhar, as a recruiting officer, presumably had to gain the confidence of local justices of the peace and the friendship of townspeople even while he spent money, cajoled, and tricked young men into military service. Despite his own precarious financial condition at the time, he spent

[10] Willard Connely, *Young George Farquhar* (London, 1949), is the standard biography.

[11] See the scholarly edition of *Mes Rêveries*, ed. Henri Charles-Lavauzelle (Paris, 1895), pp. 1–2. The work has been translated by Thomas Phillips as *Reveries on the Art of War* (Harrisburg, Pa., 1944); see pp. 22–23.

money freely to entice recruits. Though Orrery observed Farquhar's recruiting successes with pleasure, he noticed with some apprehension that Farquhar spent his own limited funds too liberally.

The Recruiting Officer, which re-established Farquhar's reputation as a successful dramatist after the relative unpopularity of his plays between 1701 and 1706, was thus highly topical. It continues to be an amusing, informative, first-hand account of the recruitment of soldiers for Queen Anne's army in the War of the Spanish Succession under the Mutiny and Impressment Acts of 1703, 1704, and 1705. Those Acts provided that debtors and even convicted felons might be released from prison if they would agree to serve in the army or navy. More relevant to *The Recruiting Officer*, justices of the peace were empowered to raise and levy able-bodied men who had no lawful calling, employment, or visible means for their maintenance and livelihood to serve as soldiers. Farquhar demonstrates, in the machinations of Sergeant Kite, Captain Plume, and Squire Balance, that the Acts could easily be used to ensnare innocent men into forced service. When Kite gains a collier for Captain Plume's company by reminding Justice Balance that the coal miner "has no visible means of livelihood, for he works underground," Farquhar humorously and yet realistically reports on a social injustice of his day. But Farquhar exposes, too, the woman brought to court with her "husband": "We agreed," she explains, "that I should call him husband to avoid passing for a whore, and that he should call me wife to shun going for a soldier." If Farquhar pictures his society accurately, his wit and good humor transform a potentially unpleasant situation into comedy.

Farquhar did not intend to focus on the social ills of impressment; he was not concerned with social reform. He wrote to entertain his audience, to delight rather than to instruct. And he chose in large part to reach his goal by using themes and devices which had proved successful either in his earlier plays or in the plays of such brilliant predecessors as Wycherley, Etherege, Vanbrugh, and Congreve—plays which as a former actor he knew well.

He used, for example, in Silvia's impersonation of men, the familiar "breeches" role, a popular stage device most notably employed by Shakespeare in *Twelfth Night*, but used frequently on the Restoration stage. In *The Plain Dealer* Wycherley had introduced the character of Fidelia, a young woman who loved Manly so much that she followed him to sea disguised as a young man. Mrs. Aphra Behn, too, in *The Younger Brother* added complexity to her plot by allowing Olivia and Teresa to dress in men's clothing in order to win the hearts of Welborn and George. Farquhar himself had used the device at least twice previously: in *Love and a Bottle* (1698) when Leanthe disguised herself as Lucinda's page in order to learn more about her beloved Roebuck, and in *The Inconstant* (1702) when Oriana dressed first as a nun and later as a boy so that she might win young Mirabel.

Sergeant Kite's impersonation of an astrologer and fortune-teller (IV.iii) again shows Farquhar's employment of previously successful stage tricks. Kite's part has traditionally been popular with actors and audiences: his double talk, his sly predictions, the mumbo-jumbo of his conjurations, and the extravagance of his dress make his role most appealing. His cunning gregariousness can win a recruit with promises of future greatness and booty. Congreve had anticipated Kite by introducing Foresight in *Love for Love* as a pretender to astrology and palmistry, and so had even earlier the Earl of Orrery in *Guzman* with Francisco, "A Poetical Conjurer" who pretends to be Alcanzar "in his Conjuring-habit."

If the brilliant wit of Restoration comedy at its best turns up only infrequently in the conversation of Captain Plume and Silvia, the lively interest in financially successful marriages and the associated intrigues of lovers which Farquhar presents in *The Recruiting Officer* were common visitors to the Restoration theater. Indeed, the desire for an advantageous marriage might be said to be the central preoccupation of Restoration comedy. No other activity counted so much as the search for wealth and station in a mate. The problems involved in such a search provided the principal complications in the comedies of the period.

The clever, intellectual, often brittle wit of Restoration comedy, however, gives way in *The Recruiting Officer* to a more natural and an easier kind of humor. If Farquhar's characters less frequently speak in epigrams, if they less often discuss the world of fashion and society, they seem more human, more natural, more credible than the glittering conversationalists of the Restoration drawing room. Farquhar did not reject *in toto* Restoration conventions of characterization and turn to tender sentiments, but he nonetheless took a step toward the sentimental drama of the eighteenth century by modifying the hardness of the dramatic characters of Wycherley and his kind, a hardness that fascinates the viewer and reader of Restoration plays even as it puts him off.

The sparkle of Restoration wit has not entirely disappeared. Silvia's sauciness before her father in the trial scene and her braggadacio as Captain Pinch and Jack Wilful, as well as Plume's cocksure gallantries early in the play, give it many breezy, witty moments, although these scenes are charged with an affability that is often missing in previous comedy. Silvia's attempts to trick her father into giving his permission for her marriage and Melinda's proud disdain of Worthy approximate the prudential attitudes of Restoration drama, in which men and women are marriageable commodities. Perhaps the country atmosphere gives wider scope to Farquhar's characters. Certainly such episodes as Plume's revelation to Silvia that he is not so much the coxcomb in fact as in appearance mellow the play: "I'm not that rake that the world imagines. I have got an air of freedom which people mistake for lewdness in me as they mistake formality in others for religion." Through Plume the audience sees, too, that Silvia does not suffer from "the ingratitude, dissimulation, envy, pride, avarice, and vanity of her sister females." Melinda and Worthy also come to a genuine understanding of one another because they recognize and admit their faults to each other. These people have their faults; some, in fact, like Brazen, who is a walking folly, exemplify Restoration caricature. But most of Farquhar's major characters have a real concern for one another, a respect and affection that add dimension to them. Even loutish, foolish Bullock *does* care about his sister, Rose. The play owes much in its tone and manner of characterization to Restoration comedy, but it possesses a humanity and charm in its people and situations that are not typical of Wycherley and Etherege.

Structurally, Farquhar's play is an extraordinarily busy one. Three plots are interwoven to make its fabric. The first traces Captain Plume's efforts to enlist men for the army, efforts mightily aided by the crafty Sergeant Kite, whose tricks, including his personification of an astrologer, charm and cajole the Shropshire lads into the Queen's Grenadiers. The enlistment practices, indeed, provide much of the humor in the play. Plume's and Kite's successes in recruitment are wittily measured against the empty boasts of Captain Brazen, who has failed to recruit a single man, much less meet his quota. The other two threads of the plot are romantic. Plume courts Silvia, who, in turn, disguises herself as a rakish young recruit to test his affection for her and to win her father's permission to marry him, a difficult task since Plume has no fortune to match hers. The third plot line concerns Melinda, the country heiress. Worthy tries to win her despite the obstacles which her inheritance of twenty thousand pounds has put in his way. He fears that the young heiress, blinded by a pride induced by her new wealth, will succumb to the foolish advances of Captain Brazen. Lucy, Melinda's maid, complicates matters when she attempts to win Brazen by pretending to be her mistress. Farquhar handles the complicated threads of these three plots with dexterity and good humor. Mistaken identities, disguises assumed not only by Silvia but also by Kite and Lucy, forged letters—all complicate the play and leave many knots to be unraveled before the final curtain falls.

Farquhar's greatest contribution to the early eighteenth-century theater, however, was not his adaptation of familiar dramatic techniques nor his skillful plotting, but his use of a country setting and his appreciation of rural life. William Archer succinctly described his innovation in his two great plays, *The Recruiting Officer* and *The Beaux' Stratagem*:

> Farquhar broke away altogether from the purlieus of Covent Garden, and took comedy out into the highways and byways. . . . Farquhar introduced us to the life of the inn, the market-place, and the manor house. He showed us the squire, the justice, the innkeeper, the highwayman, the recruiting sergeant, the charitable lady, the country belle, the chambermaid, and half a score of excellent rustic types.[12]

Removing the setting of the play from London to Shrewsbury and dealing sympathetically with rural characters like Silvia, Balance, Worthy, Melinda, and even Rose gave a new dimension to Farquhar's comedy. As John Loftis states, "Farquhar's last two plays provide the single instance of appreciative treatment of rusticity; there is in fact no parallel to them until Charles Johnson's work of the second decade of the century."[13] Farquhar's experiences as a recruiting officer in Lichfield and Shrewsbury encouraged him to let new air into the theater by way of an accurate representation of a society not confined to the drawing rooms of fashionable London. His portrayal of

[12] William Archer, *George Farquhar* (London, 1906), p. 24.
[13] John Loftis, *Comedy and Society from Congreve to Fielding* (Stanford, 1959), p. 44.

country life, based on personal observation, adds a charm and fresh-ness to *The Recruiting Officer* that account in no small part for its continuing popularity. His dedication of the play to "All Friends round the Wrekin [a hill near Shrewsbury]" testifies to the affection with which he viewed the country folk he had known in 1705 and 1706: "The entertainment I found in Shropshire," he wrote, "com-mands me to be grateful, and that's all I intend." He may have duped and bribed rustics, in the manner of the wily Kite and Plume, into joining the Grenadiers, but he retained respect and admiration for the people of Shrewsbury. He invites them to laugh at his comedy, to see themselves portrayed sympathetically and not merely as fools and louts on exhibition before civilized society.

Particularly in its use of country setting, *The Recruiting Officer* anticipates Farquhar's comic masterpiece, *The Beaux' Stratagem*. In the latter play Farquhar shifts the scene from London to the country, this time to Lichfield, where he had first served as a recruiting officer. The inns, the market place, and the country houses again provide backdrops for the good-humored pursuit of love and position in marriage. And from Plume, who respects Silvia's mind and virtue, develops Aimwell, who reveals his deceit to Dorinda out of admiration for her goodness. The caricatures are still evident: Foigard, the priest with a heavy Irish accent, and Squire Sullen, the sot. But again the country principals, Dorinda and Mrs. Sullen, are depicted with sympathy and understanding. Even echoes of recruiting and impress-ment run through *The Beaux' Stratagem* and remind one of Farquhar's earlier triumph.

The fact that Farquhar wrote *The Recruiting Officer* in haste and high spirits within a few weeks can be corroborated by evidence within the play. Fast-paced and complicated, the play shows signs of unresolved difficulties in plot. Robert L. Hough has isolated three examples of such difficulties—errors which do not, however, diminish the effectiveness of the comedy.[14]

In the fourth act we learn that Lucy has been writing letters to Captain Brazen in her own hand and signing Melinda's name in the hope of trapping him into marriage. Yet in the fifth act Lucy uses Melinda's signature, which she has stolen at the fortune-teller's, to arrange an elopement with Brazen. Lucy has no reason to change

[14] Robert L. Hough, "An Error in 'The Recruiting Officer,'" *N & Q*, CXCVIII (August, 1953), pp. 340–341; and "Farquhar: 'The Recruiting Officer,'" *N & Q*, New Series, I (November, 1954), p. 454.

signatures, since she does not suspect that her plot has been detected; she has, on the contrary, every reason not to change them, because if she should do so, Brazen might notice the difference between them. Of course, Farquhar had good reason for Lucy's inconsistent action. He allows the letter with Melinda's real signature to fall into the hands of Captain Plume, who, seeing the authentic signature, speedily sends Worthy, Melinda's true lover, off to prevent what he thinks is the impending marriage of Melinda and Brazen. Worthy arrives at just the right moment to save Brazen from marriage with the disguised Lucy. Farquhar, apparently intent on keeping the suspense high until the very end of the play, never acknowledged the logical inconsistency in Lucy's action, for the error is not corrected in the second or third quarto.

The other examples of flaws in the plot are even more interesting. In the second scene of the third act, Silvia, now disguised as a young man in her brother's white suit trimmed with silver, encounters Captain Plume and claims that she is Jack Wilful. Plume enlists her and throughout this scene and a later one (IV.ii) knows her only as Wilful. Then in the second scene of the fifth act Silvia is brought into court and, still disguised, tells her father that she is Captain Pinch, a London rake. Later she is brought into court again, and her father refers to her as Pinch. This time Plume is present and, despite the fact that he has never heard the name "Pinch" before and has already enlisted Silvia as Wilful, makes no comment when the Justice insists on her enlistment as Pinch. Farquhar apparently forgot that Plume knew her only as Wilful. Still later (V.vii), he makes exactly the opposite mistake when he has Balance speak of Silvia as Wilful, although the Justice has never heard this name before and knows her only as Pinch.

Despite these minor flaws, *The Recruiting Officer* plays extremely well. Certainly the audience watching the production is not bothered by and, indeed, probably never notices these results of Farquhar's haste. The imperfections of the plot derive from his attempt to enrich the fabric of the play and to enliven it with new opportunities for maintaining suspense. And judging from the reception given to the comedy, his efforts were well worth while.

Christopher Rich put *The Recruiting Officer* into rehearsal in late February or March, 1706, assembling a distinguished cast which included Farquhar's old friend Robert Wilks as Plume, Colley

Cibber as Brazen, Anne Oldfield as Silvia, and Richard Estcourt as Kite.[15] The play opened at the Theatre Royal in Drury Lane on April 8, 1706, to an enthusiastic audience whose applause assured a successful run. Farquhar's first benefit came the third of five performances that week; and he had two further benefits the next week.[16] Two performances in June and a special performance in Bath in September demonstrated the play's continuing popularity.[17]

The battle of the theaters in the fall and winter of 1706 shows how completely *The Recruiting Officer* had succeeded. Several members of Rich's company at Drury Lane left him in the fall to play with Owen Swiney at the Haymarket. Rich, however, picked up the remnants of his company and on October 24 opened his season in Dorset Garden, billing his players as the Drury Lane Company, with *The Recruiting Officer*.[18] He repeated the play on November 1 and 30 and December 7. The deserters to the Haymarket Theatre, including Wilks and Anne Oldfield, defied Rich by playing the comedy on the nights of November 14 and 18, and in opposition on November 30. The feud continued throughout December, with Swiney playing *The Recruiting Officer* on December 19 and 28.[19] If Rich could boast that in Estcourt he still had the original Sergeant Kite, Swiney could advertise the original Plume and Silvia. Ironically, Farquhar, who was in desperate need of money, received nothing from the frequent performances of his comedy.

Almost at once it became a stock comedy played at the beginning of each season while players learned new roles. "Opening in September," Emmett Avery explains, "each house acted twice or thrice weekly the best stock plays—*Hamlet*, *Othello*, *The Recruiting Officer*, *The Stratagem*, *Love for Love*."[20] Farquhar's play retained its popularity throughout the century. It was presented, in all, 447 times between 1706 and 1776 without missing a single season, a distinguished record that testifies to its enduring charm. On two occasions in the century it was chosen to inaugurate new theaters: the New Lincoln's Inn Fields in 1714, and the theater in Goodman's Fields in 1728.[21]

[15] The *Dramatis Personae* of Q1–3 gives the cast of the first night's performance.

[16] Avery, *The London Stage*, I, 122–123.

[17] *Ibid.*, p. 126.   [18] *Ibid.*, pp. 129–130.

[19] *Ibid.*, pp. 131–136.

[20] *Ibid.*, p. cxii.

[21] *Ibid.*, p. xxxii; Arthur H. Scouten, *The London Stage 1660–1800, Part Three: 1729–1747* (Carbondale, Ill., 1961), I, lvii.

Londoners even saw a French version of the play, *L'Officier en Recrue*, in the season of 1749–1750.[22] Charles Kemble presented the play at the Haymarket in 1797 and at Covent Garden in 1812 and again in 1819. Throughout the nineteenth century *The Recruiting Officer* remained one of the most popular plays in the repertory of provincial companies.[23]

In our century, revivals such as the fifty-six performances with Trevor Howard as Captain Plume presented by the Arts Theatre in London between November, 1943, and January, 1944, help one to see the play not only as a historical curiosity or as a bridge between the Restoration drama and the sentimental drama of the eighteenth century, but as part of the living theater. Sir Laurence Olivier's happy decision in 1963 to mount a new production of *The Recruiting Officer* under the direction of William Gaskill for the first season of Great Britain's new National Theatre marks the latest testament to its dramatic effectiveness. Its intricate plot, delightful situations, and refreshing and natural humor have appealed to every age.

I should like to thank Professor Benjamin Boyce for his examination of a first edition of the play in the British Museum and Professor William McBurney and Mr. Carl A. Barth for their thoughtful suggestions about the text and introduction.

MICHAEL SHUGRUE

University of Illinois

[22] George Winchester Stone, *The London Stage 1660–1800, Part Four: 1747–1776* (Carbondale, Ill., 1962), I, 174.

[23] Charles Stonehill, *The Complete Works of George Farquhar* (Bloomsbury, 1930), II, 39.

THE RECRUITING OFFICER

Captique dolis, donisque coacti.
Virg. Lib. II *Aeneid.*

Captured with tricks and brought together
with gifts.

Captique . . . coacti] A paraphrase of *captique dolis lacrimisque coactis* (*Aeneid*, II, 196), "captured with tricks and forced tears."

THE EPISTLE DEDICATORY

To All Friends round the Wrekin.

MY LORDS AND GENTLEMEN,

Instead of the mercenary expectations that attend
addresses of this nature, I humbly beg that this may be 5
received as an acknowledgment for the favors you have
already conferred. I have transgressed the rules of dedication in offering you anything in that style without first
asking your leave, but the entertainment I found in
Shropshire commands me to be grateful, and that's all I 10
intend.

'Twas my good fortune to be ordered some time ago
into the place which is made the scene of this comedy. I
was a perfect stranger to everything in Salop but its
character of loyalty, the number of its inhabitants, the 15
alacrity of the gentlemen in recruiting the army, with their
generous and hospitable reception of strangers.

This character I found so amply verified in every
particular that you made recruiting, which is the greatest
fatigue upon earth to others, to be the greatest pleasure in 20
the world to me.

The kingdom cannot show better bodies of men, better
inclinations for the service, more generosity, more good
understanding, nor more politeness than is to be found at
the foot of the Wrekin. 25

Some little turns of humor that I met with almost
within the shade of that famous hill gave rise to this comedy,
and people were apprehensive that, by the example of some
others, I would make the town merry at the expense of the
country gentlemen. But they forgot that I was to write a 30
comedy, not a libel; and that whilst I held to nature, no
person of any character in your country could suffer by
being exposed. I have drawn the justice and the clown in

2. Wrekin] *Corrected from "Rekin"*   *Errata Q1.*
throughout the Epistle Dedicatory in the

---

2. *Wrekin*] an isolated peak near Shrewsbury.
14. *Salop*] Shropshire; Shrewsbury is the county seat.

their *puris naturalibus*: the one an apprehensive, sturdy, brave blockhead; and the other a worthy, honest, generous 35 gentleman, hearty in his country's cause, and of as good an understanding as I could give him, which I must confess is far short of his own.

I humbly beg leave to interline a word or two of the adventures of the *Recruiting Officer* upon the stage. Mr. Rich, 40 who commands the company for which those recruits were raised, has desired me to acquit him before the world of a charge which he thinks lies heavy upon him for acting this play on Mr. Durfey's third night.

Be it known unto all men by these presents that it was my 45 act and deed, or rather Mr. Durfey's, for he would play his third night against the first of mine. He brought down a huge flight of frightful birds upon me, when heaven knows I had not a feathered fowl in my play except one single *Kite*. But I presently made *Plume* a bird, because of his name, and 50 *Brazen* another, because of the feather in his hat, and with these three I engaged his whole empire, which I think was as great a wonder as any in the sun.

But to answer his complaints more gravely, the season was far advanced; the officers that made the greatest figures in 55 my play were all commanded to their posts abroad, and waited only for a wind which might possibly turn in less time than a day. And I know none of Mr. Durfey's birds that had posts abroad but his woodcocks, and their season is over, so that he might put off a day with less prejudice than 60 the *Recruiting Officer* could, who has this farther to say for himself, that he was posted before the other spoke and could not with credit recede from his station.

These and some other rubs this comedy met with before it appeared. But on the other hand, it had powerful helps to 65 see it forward. The Duke of Ormonde encouraged the author, and the Earl of Orrery approved the play. My recruits were reviewed by my general and my colonel and

---

34. *puris naturalibus*] in the natural state.
44. *Mr. . . . night*] Thomas Durfey's *Wonders in the Sun, or the Kingdom of the Birds*, a burlesque opera, opened at the Queen's Theater, Haymarket, on April 5, 1706. The third performance, on April 8, was Durfey's benefit.

could not fail to pass muster. And still to add to my success, they were raised among my friends round the Wrekin.   70

This health has the advantage over our other celebrated toasts never to grow worse for the wearing; 'tis a lasting beauty, old without age, and common without scandal. That you may live long to let it cheerfully round and to enjoy the abundant pleasures of your fair and plentiful   75 country is the hearty wish of,

My Lords and Gentlemen,
Your most obliged,
and most obedient servant,
GEORGE FARQUHAR   80

THE PROLOGUE

In ancient times, when Helen's fatal charms
Rous'd the contending universe to arms,
The Grecian Council happily deputes
The sly Ulysses forth to raise recruits.
The artful captain found, without delay,   5
Where great Achilles, a deserter, lay.
Him Fate had warn'd to shun the Trojan blows;
Him Greece requir'd against their Trojan foes.
All the recruiting arts were needful here
To raise this great, this tim'rous volunteer.   10
Ulysses well could talk. He stirs, he warns
The warlike youth. He listens to the charms
Of plunder, fine lac'd coats, and glitt'ring arms.
Ulysses caught the young, aspiring boy,
And listed him who wrought the fate of Troy.   15
Thus by recruiting was bold Hector slain;
Recruiting thus fair Helen did regain.
If for one Helen such prodigious things
Were acted, that they ev'n listed kings;
If for one Helen's artful, vicious charms   20
Half the transported world was found in arms;
What for so many Helens may we dare
Whose minds, as well as faces, are so fair?
If, by one Helen's eyes, old Greece could find
Its Homer fired to write, ev'n Homer blind,   25
The Britains sure beyond compare may write,
That view so many Helens every night.

EPILOGUE

All ladies and gentlemen that are willing to see the comedy called *The Recruiting Officer*, let them repair tomorrow night by six o'clock to the sign of the Theatre Royal in Drury Lane, and they shall be kindly entertained.

> We scorn the vulgar ways to bid you come,　　　　5
> Whole Europe now obeys the call of drum.
> The soldier, not the poet, here appears,
> And beats up for a corps of volunteers.
> He finds that music chiefly does delight ye,
> And therefore chooses music to invite ye.　　　10

Beat the *Grenadier March*—Row, row, tow—Gentlemen, this piece of music, called an *Overture to a Battle*, was composed by a famous Italian master, and was performed with wonderful success at the great operas of Vigo, Schellenberg, and Blenheim. It came off with the applause of all Europe,　15 excepting France; the French found it a little too rough for their *delicatesse*.

> Some that have acted on those glorious stages,
> Are here to witness to succeeding ages,
> That no music like the *Grenadier's* engages.　　20

Ladies, we must own that this music of ours is not altogether so soft as Bononcini's, yet we dare affirm that it had laid more people asleep than all the *Camillas* in the world; and you'll condescend to own that it keeps one awake better than any opera that ever was acted.　　25

The *Grenadier March* seems to be a composure excellently adapted to the genius of the English, for no music was ever followed so far by us, nor with so much alacrity. And with all deference to the present subscription, we must say that

---

11. *Grenadier March*] a popular march printed as early as 1686 in Playford's *Dancing Master*.

14–15. *Vigo, . . . Blenheim*] scenes of three English victories between 1702 and 1704.

22. *Bononcini*] Marc Antonio Bononcini composed the music for the opera *Camilla*, which was performed unsuccessfully at Drury Lane on March 30, 1706.

the *Grenadier March* has been subscribed for by the whole   30
Grand Alliance; and we presume to inform the ladies that
it always has the pre-eminence abroad, and is constantly
heard by the tallest, handsomest men in the whole army. In
short, to gratify the present taste, our author is now adapting
some words to the *Grenadier March* which he intends to have   35
performed tomorrow, if the lady who is to sing it should not
happen to be sick.

This he concludes to be the surest way
To draw you hither, for you'll all obey
Soft music's call, though you should damn his play.   40

---

31. *Grand Alliance*] included the Holy Roman Empire, Holland, England,
Spain, and Saxony united against France.

Dramatis Personae

MEN

Mr. Balance, *country squire and justice of the peace*	*Mr. Keen*
Mr. Scale, *justice of the peace*	*Mr. Phillips*
Mr. Scruple, *justice of the peace*	*Mr. Kent*
Mr. Worthy, *Shropshire gentleman*	*Mr. Williams*
Captain Plume, *recruiting officer*	*Mr. Wilks*
Captain Brazen, *recruiting officer*	*Mr. Cibber*
Kite, *sergeant to Plume*	*Mr. Estcourt*
Bullock, *country lad*	*Mr. Bullock*
Costar Pearmain, *recruit*	*Mr. Norris*
Thomas Appletree, *recruit*	*Mr. Fairbank*
Butcher, *recruit*	
Smith, *recruit*	
Constable	

WOMEN

Melinda, *Shropshire lady of fortune*	*Mrs. Rogers*
Silvia, *daughter to Balance, in love with Plume*	*Mrs. Oldfield*
Lucy, *Melinda's maid*	*Mrs. Sapsford*
Rose, *Bullock's sister*	*Mrs. Monntfort*

Recruits, Servants, Attendants, and Mob

Scene, *Shrewsbury*

The Recruiting Officer

ACT I

[I.i]   *The marketplace.*
Drum beats the Grenadier March. Enter Sergeant Kite *followed by the Mob.*

KITE (*making a speech*).

If any gentlemen soldiers or others have a mind to serve her
Majesty and pull down the French king, if any 'prentices
have severe masters, any children have undutiful parents, if
any servants have too little wages, or any husband too much
wife, let them repair to the noble Sergeant Kite at the Sign   5
of the Raven in this good town of Shrewsbury and they shall
receive present relief and entertainment.

Gentlemen, I don't beat my drums here to ensnare or
inveigle any man; for you must know, gentlemen, that I am
a man of honor. Besides, I don't beat up for common   10
soldiers. No, I list only grenadiers, grenadiers, gentlemen.
Pray, gentlemen, observe this cap. This is the cap of honor;
it dubs a man a gentleman in the drawing of a tricker; and
he that has the good fortune to be born six foot high was born
to be a great man. (*To one of the Mob.*)   Sir, will you give   15
me leave to try this cap upon your head?

MOB.

Is there no harm in't? Won't the cap list me?

KITE.

No, no, no more than I can. Come, let me see how it
becomes you.

MOB.

Are you sure there be no conjuration in it, no gunpowder   20
plot upon me?

15. S.D.] *om.* Q2–3.

---

13. *tricker*] trigger.
17. *Mob.*] Archer assigns these speeches to Costar Pearmain.

KITE.

No, no, friend; don't fear, man.

MOB.

My mind misgives me plaguely. Let me see it. (*Going to put it on.*) It smells woundily of sweat and brimstone. Pray, Sergeant, what writing is this upon the face of it?   25

KITE.

The crown, or the bed of honor.

MOB.

Pray now, what may be that same bed of honor?

KITE.

Oh, a mighty large bed, bigger by half than the great bed of Ware. Ten thousand people may lie in't together and never feel one another.   30

MOB.

My wife and I would do well to lie in't, for we don't care for feeling one another. But do folk sleep sound in this same bed of honor?

KITE.

Sound! Ay, so sound that they never wake.

MOB.

Wauns! I wish again that my wife lay there.   35

KITE.

Say you so? Then I find, brother—

MOB.

Brother! Hold there, friend, I'm no kindred to you that I know of as yet. Look'e, Sergeant, no coaxing, no wheedling, d'ye'see. If I have a mind to list, why so; if not, why 'tis not so. Therefore, take your cap and your brothership back   40 again, for I an't disposed at this present writing. No coaxing, no brothering me, faith.

28. S.P. KITE] Serj. *Q1, as in ll. 34,*   37. I'm] *Q1*; I am *Q2–3*.
36.   38. as yet] *Q1*; yet *Q2–3*.
29. in't] *Q1*; in it *Q2–3*.   41. an't] *Q1*; am not *Q2–3*.
34. wake] *Q1–2*; awake *Q3*.

---

26. *crown*] The badge of the Grenadier Guards was the crown above the royal cipher or monogram. The cipher varied with the reign.

28–29. *bed of Ware*] Shakespeare in *Twelfth Night* and Byron in *Don Juan* also make reference to this famous bed, which was twelve feet square and said to be capable of accommodating twenty-four people.

KITE.

> I coax! I wheedle! I'm above it. Sir, I have served twenty
> campaigns. But, sir, you talk well, and I must own that you
> are a man every inch of you, a pretty, young, sprightly   45
> fellow. I love a fellow with a spirit, but I scorn to coax, 'tis
> base; though I must say that never in my life have I seen a
> better built man. How firm and strong he treads; he steps
> like a castle! But I scorn to wheedle any man. Come,
> honest lad, will you take share of a pot?   50

MOB.

> Nay, for that matter, I'll spend my penny with the best he
> that wears a head, that is begging you pardon, sir, and in a
> fair way.

KITE.

> Give me your hand then, and now, gentlemen, I have no
> more to say but this. Here's a purse of gold, and there is a   55
> tub of humming ale at my quarters; 'tis the Queen's money
> and the Queen's drink. She's a generous Queen and loves
> her subjects. I hope, gentlemen, you won't refuse the
> Queen's health?

ALL MOB.

> No, no, no.   60

KITE.

> Huzza then, huzza for the Queen and the honor of
> Shropshire.

ALL MOB.

> Huzza.

KITE.

> Beat drum.   *Exeunt, drum beating the Grenadier March.*

Enter Plume *in a riding habit.*

PLUME.

> By the Grenadier March that should be my drum and by   65
> that shout it should beat with success. Let me see. (*Looks
> on his watch.*)   Four o'clock. At ten yesterday morning I left
> London. A hundred and twenty miles in thirty hours is
> pretty smart riding, but nothing to the fatigue of recruiting.

---

48. better built man] *Q1*; man   64. S.D.   *the   Grenadier*]   *Q1*;   *a*
better built *Q2–3*.   *Grenadier's Q2–3.*

Enter Kite.

KITE.

Welcome to Shrewsbury, noble Captain; from the banks of 70
the Danube to the Severn side, noble Captain, you are
welcome.

PLUME.

A very elegant reception indeed, Mr. Kite. I find you are
fairly entered into your recruiting strain. Pray, what
success? 75

KITE.

I have been here but a week and I have recruited five.

PLUME.

Five! Pray, what are they?

KITE.

I have listed the strong man of Kent, the king of the gypsies,
a Scotch peddler, a scoundrel attorney, and a Welsh parson.

PLUME.

An attorney! Wer't thou mad? List a lawyer! Discharge 80
him, discharge him this minute.

KITE.

Why, sir?

PLUME.

Because I will have nobody in my company that can write.
A fellow that can write can draw petitions. I say, this
minute discharge him. 85

KITE.

And what shall I do with the parson?

PLUME.

Can he write?

KITE.

Umh.—He plays rarely upon the fiddle.

PLUME.

Keep him, by all means. But how stands the country

71. you are] *Q1*; you're *Q2–3*.

---

71. *Danube*] Plume has come to Shrewsbury from Germany and the
Battle of Blenheim.
78. *strong man of Kent*] William Joy, calling himself Samson, a Kentish
strong man, leased Dorset Garden Theatre in 1699.

affected? Were the people pleased with the news of my   90
coming to town?

KITE.

Sir, the mob are so pleased with your honor and the justices
and better sort of people are so delighted with me that we
shall soon do our business. But, sir, you have got a recruit
here that you little think of.   95

PLUME.

Who?

KITE.

One that you beat up for last time you were in the country.
You remember your old friend Molly at the Castle?

PLUME.

She's not with child, I hope.

KITE.

No, no, sir. She was brought to bed yesterday.   100

PLUME.

Kite, you must father the child.

KITE.

Humph. And so her friends will oblige me to marry the
mother.

PLUME.

If they should, we'll take her with us. She can wash, you
know, and make a bed upon occasion.   105

KITE.

Ay, or unmake it upon occasion, but your honor knows that
I'm married already.

PLUME.

To how many?

KITE.

I can't tell readily. I have set them down here upon the
back of the muster roll. (*Draws out the muster roll.*) Let me 110
see. *Imprimis*, Mrs. Sheely Snickereyes; she sells potatoes
upon Ormond-Key in Dublin; Peggy Guzzle, the brandy
woman at the Horse-Guard at Whitehall; Dolly Waggon,
the carrier's daughter in Hull; Mademoiselle Van-Bottom-

---

97. last] *Q1*; the last *Q2-3*.
102. Humph] *Q1*; *om. Q2-3*.
104. they] *Q2-3*; She *Q1*.

110. S.D. *Draws ... roll*] *Q1*;
draws it out Q2-3.
114. in] *Q1*; at *Q2-3*.

flat at the Buss. Then Jenny Oakam the ship-carpenter's 115
widow at Portsmouth, but I don't reckon upon her, for she
was married at the same time to two lieutenants of marines
and a man of war's boatswain.

PLUME.

A full company. You have named five. Come, make 'em
half a dozen, Kite. Is the child a boy or a girl?   120

KITE.

A chopping boy.

PLUME.

Then set the mother down in your list and the boy in mine.
Enter him a grenadier by the name of Francis Kite, absent
upon furlough. I'll allow you a man's pay for his subsistence,
and go comfort the wench in the straw.   125

KITE.

I shall, sir.

PLUME.

But hold, have you made any use of your German doctor's
habit since you arrived?

KITE.

Yes, yes, sir, and my fame's all about the country for the
most famous fortune-teller that ever told a lie. I was obliged 130
to let my landlord into the secret for the convenience of
keeping it so, but he's an honest fellow and will be trusty
to any roguery that is confided to him. This device, sir, will
get you men and me money, which I think is all we want at
present. But yonder comes your friend, Mr. Worthy. Has 135
your honor any further commands?

PLUME.

None at present.   *Exit* Kite.
'Tis indeed the picture of Worthy, but the life's departed.

Enter Worthy.

PLUME.

What! Arms-across, Worthy! Methinks you should hold
'em open when a friend's so near. The man has got the 140
vapors in his ears, I believe. I must expel this melancholy
spirit.

130. famous] *Q 1*; faithful *Q 2–3*.   133. confided] *Q 1*; trusted *Q 2–3*.
132. trusty] *Q 1*; faithful *Q 2–3*.

> Spleen, thou worst of fiends below,
> Fly, I conjure thee by this magic blow.
>
> (Slaps Worthy on the shoulder.)

WORTHY.

Plume! My dear Captain, welcome. Safe and sound 145 returned?

PLUME.

I 'scaped safe from Germany and sound, I hope, from London. You see I have lost neither leg, arm, nor nose. Then for my inside, 'tis neither troubled with sympathies nor antipathies, and I have an excellent stomach for roast beef. 150

WORTHY.

Thou art a happy fellow; once I was so.

PLUME.

What ails thee, man? No inundations nor earthquakes in Wales, I hope? Has your father rose from the dead and reassumed his estate?

WORTHY.

No. 155

PLUME.

Then you are married surely?

WORTHY.

No.

PLUME.

Then you are mad or turning Quaker.

WORTHY.

Come, I must out with it. Your once gay, roving friend is dwindled into an obsequious, thoughtful, romantic, constant 160 coxcomb.

PLUME.

And pray, what is all this for?

WORTHY.

For a woman.

PLUME.

Shake hands, brother, if you go to that. Behold me as obsequious, as thoughtful, and as constant a coxcomb as 165 your worship.

164. you] *Q1*; thou *Q2–3*.

WORTHY.

For whom?

PLUME.

For a regiment. But for a woman, 'sdeath, I have been
constant to fifteen at one time, but never melancholy for one.
And can the love of one bring you into this pickle? Pray, who   170
is this miraculous Helen?

WORTHY.

A Helen indeed, not to be won under a ten years' siege; as
great a beauty and as great a jilt.

PLUME.

A jilt! Pho, is she as great a whore?

WORTHY.

No, no.   175

PLUME.

'Tis ten thousand pities. But who is she? Do I know her?

WORTHY.

Very well.

PLUME.

Impossible. I know no woman that will hold out a ten
years' siege.

WORTHY.

What think you of Melinda?   180

PLUME.

Melinda! Why she began to capitulate this time twelve-
month, and offered to surrender upon honorable terms.
And I advised you to propose a settlement of five hundred
pound a year to her before I went last abroad.

WORTHY.

I did, and she hearkened to't, desiring only one week to   185
consider, when beyond her hopes the town was relieved
and I forced to turn my siege into a blockade.

PLUME.

Explain, explain.

WORTHY.

My Lady Richly, her aunt in Flintshire, dies and leaves her
at this critical time twenty thousand pound.   190

170. pickle] *Q1*; condition *Q2–3*.   possible *Q2–3*.
178. Impossible] *Q1*; That's im-   190. pound] *Q1*; pounds *Q2–3*.

PLUME.

Oh, the devil, what a delicate woman was there spoiled!
But by the rules of war now, Worthy, your blockade was
foolish. After such a convoy of provisions was entered the
place, you could have no thought of reducing it by famine.
You should have redoubled your attacks, taken the town by 195
storm, or have died upon the breach.

WORTHY.

I did make one general assault and pushed it with all my
forces, but I was so vigorously repulsed that, despairing of
ever gaining her for a mistress, I have altered my conduct,
given my addresses the obsequious and distant turn, and 200
court her now for a wife.

PLUME.

So, as you grew obsequious, she grew haughty, and because
you approached her as a goddess, she used you like a dog.

WORTHY.

Exactly.

PLUME.

'Tis the way of 'em all. Come Worthy, your obsequious and 205
distant airs will never bring you together. You must not
think to surmount her pride by your humility. Would you
bring her to better thoughts of you, she must be reduced to a
meaner opinion of herself. Let me see. The very first thing
that I would do should be to lie with her chambermaid and 210
hire three or four wenches in the neighborhood to report that
I had got them with child. Suppose we lampooned all the
pretty women in town and left her out? Or what if we made
a ball and forgot to invite her, with one or two of the ugliest?

WORTHY.

These would be mortifications, I must confess. But we live in 215
such a precise, dull place that we can have no balls, no
lampoons, no—

PLUME.

What! No bastards! And so many recruiting officers in town.
I thought 'twas a maxim among them to leave as many
recruits in the country as they carried out. 220

192. your] *Q1*; *om. Q2–3.*

WORTHY.

Nobody doubts your good will, noble Captain, in serving
your country with your best blood. Witness our friend Molly
at the Castle. There have been tears in town about that
business, Captain.

PLUME.

I hope Silvia has not heard of't.   225

WORTHY.

Oh, sir, have you thought of her? I began to fancy you
had forgot poor Silvia.

PLUME.

Your affairs had put my own quite out of my head. 'Tis
true Silvia and I had once agreed to go to bed together,
could we have adjusted preliminaries, but she would have 230
the wedding before consummation and I was for consummation before the wedding. We could not agree. She was a
pert, obstinate fool and would lose her maidenhead her own
way so she may keep it for Plume.

WORTHY.

But do you intend to marry upon no other conditions?   235

PLUME.

Your pardon, sir, I'll marry upon no conditions at all. If I
should, I'm resolved never to bind myself to a woman for
my whole life till I know whether I shall like her company for
half an hour. Suppose I married a woman that wanted a
leg? Such a thing might be, unless I examined the goods   240
beforehand. If people would but try one another's constitu-
tions before they engaged, it would prevent all these
elopements, divorces, and the devil knows what.

WORTHY.

Nay, for that matter, the town did not stick to say that—

PLUME.

I hate country towns for that reason. If your town has a 245
dishonorable thought of Silvia, it deserves to be burned to
the ground. I love Silvia, I admire her frank, generous
disposition. There's something in that girl more than
woman. Her sex is but a foil to her. The ingratitude, dissimulation, envy, pride, avarice, and vanity of her sister 250

225. of't] *Q1*; of it *Q2–3*.   228. my own] *Q1*; mine *Q2–3*.

females do but set off their contraries in her. In short, were I
once a general, I would marry her.

WORTHY.

Faith, you have reason, for were you but a corporal, she
would marry you. But my Melinda coquets it with every
fellow she sees. I lay fifty pound she makes love to you.   255

PLUME.

I'll lay fifty pound that I return it if she does. Look'e,
Worthy, I'll win her and give her to you afterwards.

WORTHY.

If you win her, you shall wear her, faith. I would not give a
fig for the conquest without the credit of the victory.

Enter Kite.

KITE.

Captain, Captain, a word in your ear.   260

PLUME.

You may speak out; here are none but friends.

KITE.

You know, sir, that you sent me to comfort the good woman
in the straw, Mrs. Molly, my wife, Mr. Worthy.

WORTHY.

Oho, very well. I wish you joy, Mr. Kite.

KITE.

Your worship very well may, for I have got both a wife and   265
a child in half an hour, but as I was a-saying, you sent me to
comfort Mrs. Molly, my wife, I mean. But what d'ye think,
sir? She was better comforted before I came.

PLUME.

As how?

KITE.

Why, sir, a footman in a blue livery had brought her ten   270
guineas to buy her baby clothes.

PLUME.

Who in the name of wonder could send them?

255. I lay] *Q1–2*; I'll lay *Q3*.   261. You] *Q2–3*; Your *Q1*.
258–259. give a fig for] *Q1*; value   266. a-saying] *Q1*; saying *Q2–3*.
Q2–3.

KITE.

Nay, sir, I must whisper that. (*Whispers* Plume.)   Mrs.
Silvia.

PLUME.

Silvia! Generous creature!   275

WORTHY.

Silvia! Impossible.

KITE.

Here be the guineas, sir. I took the gold as part of my wife's
portion. Nay farther, sir, she sent word that the child should
be taken all imaginable care of, and that she intended to
stand godmother. The same footman, as I was coming to you 280
with this news, called after me and told me that his lady
would speak with me. I went, and upon hearing that you
were come to town, she gave me half a guinea for the news
and ordered me to tell you that Justice Balance, her father,
who is just come out of the country, would be glad to see 285
you.

PLUME.

There's a girl for you, Worthy. Is there anything of woman
in this? No, 'tis a noble and generous, manly friendship.
Show me another woman that would lose an inch of her
prerogative that way, without tears, fits, and reproaches. 290
The common jealousy of her sex, which is nothing but their
avarice of pleasure, she despises, and can part with the lover
though she dies for the man. Come, Worthy. Where's the
best wine? For there I'll quarter.

WORTHY.

Horton has a fresh pipe of choice Barcelona which I would 295
not let him pierce before because I reserved the maidenhead
of it for your welcome to town.

PLUME.

Let's away then. Mr. Kite, wait on the lady with my humble

277. be] *Q1*; are *Q2–3*.   288. noble and generous] *Q1*;
278. that the child] *Q1*; the child   noble, generous *Q2–3*.
Q2–3.

295. *pipe*] a large wine cask with a capacity of about two hogsheads, or
126 gallons.

service and tell her that I shall only refresh a little, and wait
on her.   300
WORTHY.
Hold, Kite. Have you seen the other recruiting captain?
KITE.
No, sir.
PLUME.
Another? Who is he?
WORTHY.
My rival in the first place, and the most unaccountable
fellow. But I'll tell you more as we go.   [*Exeunt.*] 305

[I.ii]   *An apartment.*
                    [*Enter*] Melinda *and* Silvia *meeting.*
MELINDA.
Welcome to town, cousin Silvia. (*Salute.*) I envied you
your retreat in the country, for Shrewsbury, methinks, and
all your heads of shires, are the most irregular places for
living. Here we have smoke, noise, scandal, affectation, and
pretension, in short, everything to give the spleen and   5
nothing to divert it. Then the air is intolerable.
SILVIA.
Oh, madam, I have heard the town commended for its air.
MELINDA.
But you don't consider, Silvia, how long I have lived in it;
for I can assure you that to a lady the least nice in her constitution, no air can be good above half a year. Change of   10
air I take to be the most agreeable of any variety in life.
SILVIA.
As you say, cousin Melinda, there are several sorts of airs:
airs in conversation, airs in behavior, airs in dress. Then we
have our quality airs, our sickly airs, our reserved airs, and
sometimes our impudent airs.   15
MELINDA.
Pshaw, I talk only of the air we breathe, or more properly,

299. that] *Q1; om. Q2–3.*   8. in it] *Q1;* in't *Q2–3.*
300. on] *Q1;* upon *Q2–3.*   13–15. airs in conversation ...
[I.ii]   impudent airs] *Q1; om. Q2–3.*

of that we taste. Have not you, Silvia, found a vast difference
in the taste of airs?

SILVIA.

Pray, cousin, are not vapors a sort of air? Taste air? You
may as well tell me I might feed upon air. But prithee, my   20
dear Melinda, don't put on such airs to me. Your education
and mine were just the same, and I remember the time when
we never troubled our heads about air, but when the sharp
air from the Welsh mountains made our noses drop in a cold
morning at the boarding school.   25

MELINDA.

Our education, cousin, was the same, but our temperaments
had nothing alike. You have the constitution of a horse.

SILVIA.

So far as to be troubled with neither spleen, colic, nor
vapors. I need no salt for my stomach, no hartshorn for my
head, nor wash for my complexion. I can gallop all the   30
morning after the hunting horn and all the evening after a
fiddle. In short, I can do everything with my father but
drink and shoot flying, and I'm sure I can do everything my
mother could, were I put to the trial.

MELINDA.

You are in a fair way of being put to't, for I'm told your   35
captain is come to town.

SILVIA.

Ay, Melinda, he is come, and I'll take care he shan't go
without a companion.

MELINDA.

You're certainly mad, cousin.

SILVIA.

And there's a pleasure sure in being mad,   40

20. may] *Q1*; might *Q2–3*.
20. might] *Q1*; may *Q2–3*.
21. airs] *Q1*; an air *Q2–3*.
24. noses drop] *Q1*; fingers ache
Q2–3.
27. a] *Q1*; an *Q2–3*.
29. salt] *Q1*; salts *Q2–3*.

33. I'm] *Q1*; I am *Q2–3*.
35. You are] *Q2–3*; You're are *Q1*.
35. I'm] *Q1*; I am *Q2–3*.
39. You're] *Q1*; You are *Q2–3*.
40. sure] *Q1*; *om. Q2–3. The lines
are printed as prose in Q2–3.*

40–41. And ... know] Silvia quotes from John Dryden's *The Spanish
Friar* (II.i).

–23–

Which none but madmen know.

MELINDA.

Thou poor, romantic Quixote. Hast thou the vanity to imagine that a young, sprightly officer that rambles over half the globe in half a year can confine his thoughts to the little daughter of a country justice in an obscure corner of the 45 world?

SILVIA.

Pshaw! What care I for his thoughts? I should not like a man with confined thoughts; it shows a narrowness of soul. Constancy is but a dull, sleepy quality at best; they will hardly admit it among the manly virtues. Nor do I think it 50 deserves a place with bravery, knowledge, policy, justice, and some other qualities that are proper to that noble sex. In short, Melinda, I think a petticoat a mighty simple thing, and I'm heartily tired of my sex.

MELINDA.

That is, you are tired of an appendix to our sex that you 55 can't so handsomely get rid of in petticoats as if you were in breeches. O'my conscience, Silvia, hadst thou been a man, thou hadst been the greatest rake in Christendom.

SILVIA.

I should endeavor to know the world, which a man can never do thoroughly without half a hundred friendships and 60 as many amours. But now I think on't, how stands your affair with Mr. Worthy?

MELINDA.

He's my aversion.

SILVIA.

Vapors!

MELINDA.

What do you say, madam?   65

SILVIA.

I say that you should not use that honest fellow so in-humanely. He's a gentleman of parts and fortune, and beside that he's my Plume's friend, and by all that's sacred,

---

43. over] *Q1*; o'er *Q2-3*.   59. endeavor] *Q1*; have endeavored
45. corner] *Q1*; part *Q2-3*.   *Q2-3*.
54. I'm] *Q1*; I am *Q2-3*.   68. beside] *Q1*; besides *Q2-3*.

if you don't use him better, I shall expect satisfaction.

MELINDA.

Satisfaction! You begin to fancy yourself in breeches in good   70
earnest. But to be plain with you, I like Worthy the worse
for being so intimate with your captain, for I take him to be
a loose, idle, unmannerly coxcomb.

SILVIA.

Oh, madam. You never saw him, perhaps, since you were
mistress of twenty thousand pound. You only knew him   75
when you were capitulating with Worthy for a settlement
which might encourage him to be a little loose and
unmannerly with you.

MELINDA.

What do you mean, madam?

SILVIA.

My meaning needs no interpretation, madam.   80

MELINDA.

Better it had, madam, for methinks you're too plain.

SILVIA.

If you mean the plainness of my person, I think your
ladyship as plain as me to the full.

MELINDA.

Were I assured of that, I should be glad to take up with a
rakely officer as you do.   85

SILVIA.

Again! Look'e, madam, you're in your own house.

MELINDA.

And if you had kept in yours, I should have excused you.

SILVIA.

Don't be troubled, madam. I shan't desire to have my visit
returned.

MELINDA.

The sooner therefore you make an end of this, the better.   90

SILVIA.

I'm easily advised to follow my inclinations. So, madam,
your humble servant.   *Exit.*

75. pound] *Q1*; pounds *Q2–3*.
81. you're] *Q1*; you are *Q2–3*.
84. assured] *Q1*; sure *Q2–3*.

84. should] *Q1–2*; would *Q3*.
91. I'm ... advised] *Q1*; I am
easily persuaded *Q2–3*.

MELINDA.

    Saucy thing!

                    Enter Lucy.

LUCY.

    What's the matter, madam?

MELINDA.

    Did not you see the proud nothing, how she swells upon   95
    the arrival of her fellow?

LUCY.

    Her fellow has not been long enough arrived to occasion any
    great swelling, madam. I don't believe she has seen him yet.

MELINDA.

    Nor shan't if I can help it. Let me see. I have it. Bring me
    pen and ink. Hold, I'll go write in my closet.   100

LUCY.

    An answer to this letter, I hope, madam.   (*Presents a letter.*)

MELINDA.

    Who sent it?

LUCY.

    Your captain, madam.

MELINDA.

    He's a fool, and I'm tired of him. Send it back unopened.

LUCY.

    The messenger's gone, madam.   105

MELINDA.

    Then how shall I send an answer? Call him back immedi-
    ately, while I go write.   *Exeunt severally.*

ACT II

[II.i]   *An apartment.*
         Enter Justice Balance *and* Plume.

BALANCE.

    Look'e, Captain, give us but blood for our money and you
    shan't want men. I remember that for some years of the last
    war we had no blood nor wounds but in the officers' mouths,
    nothing for our millions but newspapers not worth a reading.

95. swells] *Q1*; swelled *Q2–3*.   [II.i]
106. shall] *Q1*; should *Q2–3*.   3. nor] *Q1*; no *Q2–3*.

Our armies did nothing but play at prison bars, and hide   5
and seek with the enemy, but now ye have brought us colors
and standards and prisoners. Odmylife, Captain, get us
but another Marshal of France and I'll go myself for a
soldier.

PLUME.

Pray, Mr. Balance, how does your fair daughter?   10

BALANCE.

Ah, Captain, what is my daughter to a Marshal of France.
We're upon a nobler subject. I want to have a particular
description of the battle of Hochstadt.

PLUME.

The battle, sir, was a very pretty battle as one should desire
to see, but we were all so intent upon victory that we never   15
minded the battle. All that I know of the matter is, our
general commanded us to beat the French and we did so,
and if he pleases to say the word, we'll do't again. But pray,
sir, how does Mrs. Silvia?

BALANCE.

Still upon Silvia! For shame, Captain. You're engaged   20
already, wedded to the war. War is your mistress, and it is
below a soldier to think of any other.

PLUME.

As a mistress, I confess, but as a friend, Mr. Balance?

BALANCE.

Come, come, Captain, never mince the matter. Would
not you debauch my daughter if you could?   25

PLUME.

How, sir! I hope she is not to be debauched.

BALANCE.

Faith, but she is, sir, and any woman in England of her age
and complexion, by a man of your youth and vigor. Look'e,
Captain, once I was young and once an officer as you are,
and I can guess at your thoughts now by what mine were   30

5. armies] *Q1*; army *Q2–3*.   20. You're] *Q1*; You are *Q2–3*.
17. general] *Q2–3*; generals *Q1*.   21. War] *Q1*; Victory *Q2–3*.
18. to say] *Q1*; but to say *Q2–3*.   26. she is] *Q1*; she's *Q2–3*.

11. *Marshal*] The English captured Marshal Tallard at Blenheim
(Hochstadt).

then, and I can remember very well that I would have
given one of my legs to have deluded the daughter of an old,
plain country gentleman, as like me as I was then like you.

PLUME.

But, sir, was that country gentleman your friend and
benefactor?   35

BALANCE.

Not much of that.

PLUME.

There the comparison breaks; the favors, sir, that—

BALANCE.

Pho, I hate speeches. If I have done you any service,
Captain, 'twas to please myself, for I love thee, and if I
could part with my girl, you should have her as soon as any   40
young fellow I know. But I hope you have more honor than
to quit the service, and she more prudence than to follow
the camp. But she's at her own disposal; she has fifteen
hundred pound in her pocket, and so, Silvia, Silvia.   (*Calls.*)

Enter Silvia.

SILVIA.

There are some letters, sir, come by the post from London;   45
I left them upon the table in your closet.

BALANCE.

And here is a gentleman from Germany.   (*Presents* Plume
to her.)   Captain, you'll excuse me; I'll go read my letters
and wait on you.   *Exit.*

SILVIA.

Sir, you're welcome to England.   50

PLUME.

Blessings in heaven we should receive in a prostrate
posture; let me receive my welcome thus.
                              (*Kneels and kisses her hand.*)

SILVIA.

Pray rise, sir, I'll give you fair quarter.

PLUME.

All quarter I despise; the height of conquest is to die at your
feet.   (*Kissing her hand again.*)   55

33. plain] *Q1*; *om. Q2–3*.   50. you're] *Q1*; you are *Q2–3*.
48. go read] *Q1*; go and read   51–58.] *Q1*; *see Appendix A for lines*
Q2–3.   *substituted in Q2–3*.

SILVIA.

Well, well, you shall die at my feet, or where you will, but
first let me desire you to make your will; perhaps you'll
leave me something.

PLUME.

My will, madam, is made already, and there it is. (*Gives
her a parchment*.) And if you please to open that parchment, 60
which was drawn the evening before the battle of Blenheim,
you will find whom I left my heir.

Silvia *opens the will and reads.*

SILVIA.

Mrs. Silvia Balance. Well, Captain, this is a handsome and
a substantial compliment, but I can assure you I am much
better pleased with the bare knowledge of your intention 65
than I should have been in the possession of your legacy.
But methinks, sir, you should have left something to your
little boy at the Castle.

PLUME (*aside*).

That's home. —My little boy! Lackaday, madam, that
alone may convince you 'twas none of mine. Why the girl, 70
madam, is my sergeant's wife, and so the poor creature gave
out that I was father in hopes that my friends might support
her in case of necessity; that was all, madam. My boy,
no, no.

Enter Servant.

SERVANT.

Madam, my master has received some ill news from 75
London and desires to speak with you immediately, and he
begs the Captain's pardon that he can't wait on him as he
promised.

PLUME.

Ill news! Heavens avert it; nothing could touch me nearer
than to see that generous, worthy gentleman afflicted. 80
I'll leave you to comfort him, and be assured that if my life
and fortune can be any way serviceable to the father of my
Silvia, she shall freely command both.

59–60. S.D.] *Q1*; *om. Q2–3.*   83. she] *Q1*; he *Q2–3.*
74. no, no] *Q1*; no, no, no *Q2–3.*

SILVIA.

   The necessity must be very pressing that would engage me
   to do either.   *Exeunt severally.*   85

[II.ii]   *Scene changes to another apartment.*
                         Enter Balance *and* Silvia.

SILVIA.

   Whilst there is life there is hope, sir; perhaps my brother
   may recover.

BALANCE.

   We have but little reason to expect it. Dr. Kilman acquaints
   me here that before this comes to my hands he fears I shall
   have no son. Poor Owen! But the decree is just. I was   5
   pleased with the death of my father because he left me an
   estate, and now I'm punished with the loss of an heir to
   inherit mine. I must now look upon you as the only hopes
   of my family, and I expect that the augmentation of your
   fortune will give you fresh thoughts and new prospects.   10

SILVIA.

   My desire of being punctual in my obedience requires that
   you would be plain in your commands, sir.

BALANCE.

   The death of your brother makes you sole heiress to my
   estate, which three or four years hence will amount to
   twelve hundred pound per annum. This fortune gives you a   15
   fair claim to quality and a title. You must set a just value
   upon yourself and, in plain terms, think no more of Captain
   Plume.

SILVIA.

   You have often commended the gentleman, sir.

BALANCE.

   And I do still; he's a very pretty fellow. But though I   20
   liked him well enough for a bare son-in-law, I don't approve
   of him for an heir to my estate and family. Fifteen hundred

---

85. do] *Q1*; endanger *Q2–3*.   7. I'm] *Q1*; I am *Q2–3*.
[II.ii]   14–15. which ... annum] *Q1*;
0.1. *Scene ... another*] *Q1*; *Scene,*   which you know is about twelve
another Q2–3.   hundred pounds a year *Q2–3*.
1. hope] *Q1*; hopes *Q2–3*.

pound, indeed, I might trust in his hands, and it might do
the young fellow a kindness, but odsmylife, twelve hundred
pound a year would ruin him, quite turn his brain. A   25
Captain of Foot worth twelve hundred pound a year!
'Tis a prodigy in nature. Besides this, I have five or six
thousand pounds in woods upon my estate. Oh, that would
make him stark mad, for you must know that all captains
have a mighty aversion to timber. They can't endure to see   30
trees standing. Then I should have some rogue of a builder
by the help of his damned magic art transform my noble
oaks and elms into cornices, portals, sashes, birds, beasts,
gods, and devils, to adorn some maggoty, new-fashioned
bauble upon the Thames. And then you should have a dog   35
of a gardener bring a *habeus corpus* for my *terra firma*, remove
it to Chelsea or Twitnam, and clap it into grassplots and
gravel walks.

Enter a Servant.

SERVANT.

Sir, here's one below with a letter for your worship, but he
will deliver it into no hands but your own.   40

BALANCE.

Come, show me the messenger.   *Exit with Servant.*

SILVIA.

Make the dispute between love and duty, and I am Prince
Prettyman exactly. If my brother dies, ah, poor brother; if
he lives, ah, poor sister. 'Tis bad both ways. I'll try again.
Follow my own inclinations and break my father's heart, or   45
obey his commands and break my own. Worse and worse.
Suppose I take thus—a moderate fortune, a pretty fellow
and a pad, or a fine estate, a coach-and-six, and an ass.
That will never do neither.

23, 25, 26. pound] *Q1*; pounds
Q2–3.
33–34. beasts . . . devils] *Q1*; beasts
and devils *Q2–3*.
39. here's . . . letter] *Q1*; here is one

with a letter below *Q2–3*.
44. try again] *Q1*; try it again
Q2–3.
47. take thus] *Q1*; take it thus
Q2–3.

---

37. *Chelsea or Twitnam*] Chelsea and Twickenham are London suburbs.
43. *Prettyman*] an error. Volscius—not Prettyman—in *The Rehearsal*
(III.v) is torn between the claims of love and honor.
48. *pad*] an easy-paced horse.

–31–

Enter Balance *and servant.*

BALANCE.

Put four horses into the coach.   (*To the servant, who goes out.*)   50
Silvia.

SILVIA.

Sir.

BALANCE.

How old were you when your mother died?

SILVIA.

So young that I don't remember I ever had one. And you
have been so careful, so indulgent to me since, that indeed   55
I never wanted one.

BALANCE.

Have I ever denied you anything you asked of me?

SILVIA.

Never, that I remember.

BALANCE.

Then, Silvia, I must beg that once in your life you would
grant me a favor.   60

SILVIA.

Why should you question it, sir?

BALANCE.

I don't, but I would rather counsel than command. I
don't propose this with the authority of a parent, but with
the advice of your friend, that you would take the coach this
moment and go into the country.   65

SILVIA.

Does this advice proceed from the contents of the letter you
received just now?

BALANCE.

No matter. I shall be with you in three or four days and then
give you my reasons. But before you go, I expect you will
make me one solemn promise.   70

SILVIA.

Propose the thing, sir.

BALANCE.

That you will never dispose of yourself to any man without
my consent.

50. S.D. *To the*] *Q1*; *to a Q2–3*.   66. advice] *Q1*; advice, sir *Q2–3*.
51. Silvia] *Q1*; Ho, Silvia *Q2–3*.   68. shall] *Q1*; will *Q2–3*.

SILVIA.

I promise.

BALANCE.

Very well, and to be even with you, I promise that I will   75
never dispose of you without your own consent. And so,
Silvia, the coach is ready. Farewell. (*Leads her to the door
and returns.*) Now she's gone, I'll examine the contents of
this letter a little nearer.   (*Reads.*)
"Sir,   80
My intimacy with Mr. Worthy has drawn a secret
from him that he had from his friend, Captain Plume,
and my friendship and relation to your family oblige
me to give you timely notice of it. The captain has
dishonorable designs upon my cousin Silvia. Evils of   85
this nature are more easily prevented than amended,
and that you would immediately send my cousin into
the country is the advice of,
                     Sir, your humble servant,
                              Melinda."   90
Why, the devil's in the young fellows of this age! They're
ten times worse than they were in my time. Had he made
my daughter a whore and forswore it like a gentleman, I
could have almost pardoned it, but to tell tales beforehand is monstrous! Hang it, I can fetch down a woodcock   95
or snipe, and why not a hat and feather? I have a case of
good pistols and have a good mind to try.

Enter Worthy.

BALANCE.

Worthy, your servant.

WORTHY.

I'm sorry, sir, to be the messenger of ill news.

BALANCE.

I apprehend it, sir. You have heard that my son Owen is   100
past recovery.

WORTHY.

My advices say he's dead, sir.

75–76. that . . . never] *Q1*; I never   96. or snipe] *Q1*; or a snipe *Q2–3*.
will *Q2–3*.   99. I'm] *Q1*; I am *Q2–3*.
91. They're] *Q1*; they are *Q2–3*.   102. advices] *Q1*; letters *Q2–3*.

BALANCE.

He's happy, and I am satisfied. The strokes of heaven I can
bear, but injuries from men, Mr. Worthy, are not so easily
supported.   105

WORTHY.

I hope, sir, you are under no apprehension of wrong from
anybody?

BALANCE.

You know I ought to be.

WORTHY.

You wrong my honor, sir, in believing I could know anything to your prejudice without resenting it as much as you 110
should.

BALANCE.

This letter, sir, which I tear in pieces to conceal the person
that sent it, informs me that Plume has a design upon Silvia
and that you are privy to't.

WORTHY.

Nay then, sir, I must do myself justice and endeavor to find 115
out the author. (*Takes up a piece of the letter.*)   Sir, I know
the hand, and if you refuse to discover the contents, Melinda
shall tell me.   (*Going.*)

BALANCE.

Hold, sir, the contents I have told you already, only with
this circumstance, that her intimacy with Mr. Worthy has   120
drawn the secret from him.

WORTHY.

Her intimacy with me! Dear sir, let me pick up the pieces
of this letter. 'Twill give me such a hank upon her pride to
have her own an intimacy under her hand. 'Twas the
luckiest accident. (*Gathering up the letter.*) The aspersion, 125
sir, was nothing but malice, the effect of a little quarrel
between her and Mrs. Silvia.

BALANCE.

Are you sure of that, sir?

103. I am] *Q1*; I'm *Q2–3*.   *takes up a bit Q2–3.*
106. you are] *Q1*; you're *Q2–3*.   123. hank upon] *Q1*; power over
116. S.D. *Takes ... letter*] *Q1*;   *Q2–3*.

–34–

WORTHY.

Her maid gave me the history of part of the battle just now,
as she overheard it.   130

BALANCE.

'Tis probable. I am satisfied.

WORTHY.

But I hope, sir, your daughter has suffered nothing upon
the account?

BALANCE.

No, no. Poor girl, she is so afflicted with the news of her
brother's death that to avoid company she begged leave 135
to be gone into the country.

WORTHY.

And is she gone?

BALANCE.

I could not refuse her; she was so pressing. The coach went
from the door the minute before you came.

WORTHY.

So pressing to be gone, sir. I find her fortune will give her 140
the same airs with Melinda, and then Plume and I may
laugh at one another.

BALANCE.

Like enough. Women are as subject to pride as we are,
and why mayn't great women as well as great men forget
their old acquaintance? But come, where's this young 145
fellow? I love him so well it would break the heart of me to
think him a rascal. (*Aside.*) I'm glad my daughter's
gone fairly off though. —Where does the captain quarter?

WORTHY.

At Horton's. I'm to meet him there two hours hence, and
we should be glad of your company.   150

BALANCE.

Your pardon, dear Worthy. I must allow a day or two to
the death of my son. The decorum of mourning is what we
owe the world because they pay it to us. Afterwards, I'm
yours over a bottle, or how you will.

131.] *Q1*; *om. Q2–3.*   153. to . . . I'm] to us afterwards.
134. she is] *Q1*; she's *Q2–3.*   I'm *Q1–3.*
149. I'm] *Q1*; I am *Q2–3.*

WORTHY.

    Sir, I'm your humble servant.   *Exeunt severally.* 155

[II.iii]   *The street.*
      Kite *enters with one of the* Mob *in each hand, drunk.*

KITE (*sings*).

         Our prentice Tom may now refuse
         To wipe his scoundrel master's shoes,
         For now he's free to sing and play,
         Over the hills and far away.
            Over the hills, &c.   (*The* Mob *sing the chorus.*) 5
         We all shall lead more happy lives
         By getting rid of brats and wives,
         That scold and brawl both night and day,
         Over the hills and far away.
            Over the hills, &c.   10
    Hey, boys. Thus we soldiers live, drink, dance, play; we live, as one should say. We live. 'Tis impossible to tell how we live. We're all princes. Why, why, you're a king. You're an emperor, and I'm a prince. Now, an't we?

I MOB.

    No, Sergeant, I'll be no emperor.   15

KITE.

    No?

I MOB.

    No, I'll be a justice of peace.

KITE.

    A justice of peace, man?

I MOB.

    Ay, wauns will I, for since this pressing act they are greater than any emperor under the sun.   20

0.1. *with ... mob*] *Q1*; *with a mob*
Q2–3.
5, 10. *Over ... &c.*] *Q1*; *Over,*
&c. Q2–3.

13. *We're*] *Q1*; *We are Q2–3.*
13. *you're*] *Q1*; *you are Q2–3.*
13. *You're*] *Q1*; *you are Q2–3.*

---

    5. *chorus*] Plume sings the words to the chorus, ll. 48–51.
    15. *1 Mob*] identified as Thomas Appletree later in the scene (l. 175). To avoid the confusion which exists in some speech prefixes in Q1–4, all speeches which are clearly Appletree's have been assigned to 1 Mob.

KITE.

    Done, you're a justice of peace, and you're a king, and I'm
a duke, and a rum duke, an't I?

2 MOB.

    No, but I'll be no king.

KITE.

    What then?

2 MOB.

    I'll be a queen.   25

KITE.

    A queen!

2 MOB.

    Ay, Queen of England. That's greater than any king of
'em all.

KITE.

    Bravely said, faith! Huzza for the Queen! (*All huzza.*)
But hear'e, you Mr. Justice, and you Mr. Queen, did you   30
ever see the Queen's picture?

1 AND 2 MOB.

    No, no.

KITE.

    I wonder at that; I have two of 'em set in gold, and as like
Her Majesty, God bless the mark. (*He takes two broad
pieces out of his pocket.*) See here, they're set in gold.   35
                                              (*Gives one to each.*)

1 MOB (*looking earnestly upon the piece*).

    The wonderful works of nature!

2 MOB.

    What's this written about? Here's a posy, I believe. *Ca ro*

21. you're . . . you're] *Q1*; you are   32. No, no] *Q1*; No, no, no *Q2–3*.
. . . you are *Q2–3*.   34. S.D. *He takes. two*] *Q1*; *Takes*
21. I'm] *Q1*; I am *Q2–3*.   *two Q2–3*.
23. No] *Q1*; Ay *Q2–3*.   35. they're] *Q1*; they are *Q2–3*.
29. S.D. *All huzza*] *Q1*; *huzza*   37. S.D. *looking . . . piece*] *Q1*;
Q2–3.   *looking at it Q2–3*.
31. ever] *Q1*; never *Q2–3*.

22. *rum*] fine.

23. *2 Mob*] identified as Costar Pearmain later in the scene (l. 177). To
avoid the confusion which exists in some speech prefixes in Q1–4, all
speeches which are clearly Pearmain's have been assigned to 2 Mob.

27. *Queen of England*] Queen Anne, 1702–1714.

34–35. S.D. *broad pieces*] twenty-shilling pieces from the reign of Charles
I worth twenty-three shillings and sixpence by 1706.

lus—what's that, Sergeant?

KITE.

    Oh, *Carolus*, why *Carolus* is Latin for Queen Anne, that's all.

2 MOB.

    'Tis a fine thing to be a scollard, Sergeant. Will you part   40
with this? I'll buy it on you if it come within the compass of
a crown.

KITE.

    A crown! Never talk of buying. 'Tis the same thing among
friends, you know. I present them to you both; you shall
give me as good a thing. Put them up and remember your   45
old friend, when I'm over the hills and far away.

                                             (Singing.)
                             (They sing and put up the money.)

                  Enter Plume *singing.*

PLUME.

              Over the hills, and o're the main,
              To Flanders, Portugal, or Spain;
              The Queen commands, and we'll obey,
              Over the hills and far away.   50
Come on ye men of mirth, away with it. I'll make one among
ye. Who are these hearty lads?

KITE.

    Off with your hats, wauns, off with your hats. This is the
captain, the captain.

1 MOB.

    We have seen captains before now, mun.   55

2 MOB.

    Ay, and lieutenant captains too; flesh, I'se keep on my nab.

1 MOB.

    And I'se scarcely doff mine for any captain in England.
My vether's a freeholder.

PLUME.

    Who are these jolly lads, Sergeant?

---

44. I ... them] *Q1*; I'll present   46. I'm] *Q1*; I am *Q2–3*.
'em *Q2*; I'll present them *Q3*.   56. I'se] *Q1*; I'll *Q2–3*.
45. Put them] *Q1*; Put 'em *Q2–3*.

---

56. *nab*] hat.

KITE.

A couple of honest, brave fellows that are willing to serve   60
the Queen. I have entertained them just now as volunteers
under your honor's command.

PLUME.

And good entertainment they shall have. Volunteers are
the men I want; those are the men fit to make soldiers,
captains, generals.   65

2 MOB.

Wauns, Tummas, what's this? Are you listed?

1 MOB.

Flesh, not I. Are you, Costar?

2 MOB.

Wauns, not I.

KITE.

What, not listed? Ha, ha, ha, a very good jest, faith.

2 MOB.

Come, Tummas, we'll go whome.   70

1 MOB.

Ay, ay, come.

KITE.

Home! For shame, gentlemen, behave yourselves better
before your captain. Dear Tummas, honest Costar—

2 MOB.

No, no, we'll be gone.   (*Going.*)

KITE.

Nay, then I command you to stay. I place you both sentinels   75
in this place for two hours to watch the motion of St.
Mary's clock you, and you the motion of St. Chad's. And he
that dare stir from his post till he be relieved shall have my
sword in his guts the next minute.

PLUME.

What's the matter, Sergeant? I'm afraid you're too rough   80
with these gentlemen.

KITE.

I'm too mild, sir. They disobey command, sir, and one of

61. them] *Q1*; 'em *Q2–3*.   78. dare] *Q1*; dares *Q2–3*.
70. whome] *Q1*; home *Q2–3*.   80. you're] *Q1*; you are *Q2–3*.
74. S.D. *Going*] *Q1*; *om. Q2–3*.

them should be shot for an example to the other.

2 MOB.

Shot, Tummas!

PLUME.

Come, gentlemen, what is the matter?   85

1 MOB.

We don't know. The noble sergeant is pleased to be in a
passion, sir, but—

KITE.

They disobey command; they deny their being listed.

2 MOB.

Nay, Sergeant, we don't downright deny it neither; that we
dare not do for fear of being shot, but we humbly conceive   90
in a civil way, and begging your worship's pardon, that we
may go home.

PLUME.

That's easily known. Have either of you received any of the
Queen's money?

1 MOB.

Not a brass farthing, sir.   95

KITE.

Sir, they have each of them received three and twenty
shillings and sixpence and 'tis now in their pockets.

1 MOB.

Wauns, if I have a penny in my pocket but a bent sixpence,
I'll be content to be listed, and shot into the bargain.

2 MOB.

And I, look'e here, sir.   100

1 MOB.

Ay, here's my stock too, nothing but the Queen's picture
that the sergeant gave me just now.

KITE.

See there, a broad piece, three and twenty shillings and
sixpence. The t'other has the fellow on't.

PLUME.

The case is plain, gentlemen, the goods are found upon you. 105
Those pieces of gold are worthy three and twenty and
sixpence each.

83. them] *Q1*; 'em *Q2–3*.   85. what is] *Q1*; what's *Q2–3*.

2 MOB.

So it seems that *Carolus* is three and twenty shillings and
sixpence in Latin.

I MOB.

'Tis the same thing in the Greek, for we are listed.   110

2 MOB.

Flesh, but we an't, Tummas. I desire to be carried before
the mayar, Captain.

(*While they talk, the* Captain *and* Sergeant *whisper.*)

PLUME.

'Twill never do, Kite; your damned tricks will ruin me at
last. I won't lose the fellows though, if I can help it.   Well,
gentlemen, there must be some trick in this. My sergeant 115
offers here to take his oath that you're fairly listed.

I MOB.

Why, Captain, we know that you soldiers have more liberty
of conscience than other folks, but for me or neighbor Costar
here to take such an oath 'twould be downright perjuration.

PLUME.

Look'e, you rascal, you villain, if I find that you have 120
imposed upon these two honest fellows, I'll trample you to
death, you dog. Come, how was't?

I MOB.

Nay, then we will speak. Your sergeant, as you say, is a
rogue, begging your worship's pardon, and—

2 MOB.

Nay, Tummas, let me speak. You know I can read. And 125
so, sir, he gave us those two pieces of money for pictures of
the Queen by way of a present.

PLUME.

How! By way of a present! The son of a whore! I'll teach
him to abuse honest fellows like you. Scoundrel, rogue,
villain! (*Beats the* Sergeant *off the stage and follows him out.*)   130

BOTH MOB.

O brave, noble Captain! Huzza, a brave captain, faith!

110. in   the   Greek]   *Q1–2*; in   113. tricks] *Q1*; trick *Q2–3*.
Greek *Q3*.   120. you rascal] *Q1*; rascal *Q2–3*.
112.1. *While ... whisper*] *Q1*; *Cap-*   130. villain] villain, &c. *Q1–3*.
tain and Sergeant *whisper the while*   130. *Beats ... out*] *Q1*; *beats off the*
Q2–3.   *sergeant and follows Q2–3*.

2 MOB.

> Now, Tummas, *Carolus* is Latin for a beating. This is the
> bravest captain I ever saw. Wauns, I have a month's mind
> to go with him.

Re-enter Plume.

PLUME.

> A dog, to abuse two such pretty fellows as you! Look'e,   135
> gentlemen, I love a pretty fellow. I come among you here
> as an officer to list soldiers, not as a kidnapper to steal
> slaves.

2 MOB.

> Mind that, Tummas.

PLUME.

> I desire no man to go with me but as I went myself. I went   140
> a volunteer, as you or you may go, for a little time carried
> a musket, and now I command a company.

1 MOB.

> Mind that, Costar, a sweet gentleman.

PLUME.

> 'Tis true, gentlemen, I might take an advantage of you;
> the Queen's money was in your pockets; my sergeant was   145
> ready to take his oath that you were listed, but I scorn to do
> a base thing. You are both of you at your liberty.

2 MOB.

> Thank you, noble Captain. I cod, I cannot find in my
> heart to leave him, he talks so finely.

1 MOB.

> Ay, Costar, would he always hold in this mind?   150

PLUME.

> Come, my lads, one thing more I'll tell you. You're both
> young, tight fellows and the army is the place to make you
> men forever. Every man has his lot, and you have yours.
> What think you now of a purse full of French gold out of a
> monsieur's pocket, after you have dashed out his brains   155
> with the butt of your firelock, eh?

134.1. *Re-enter*] *Q1*; *Enter Q2–3.*   146. that] *Q1*; *om. Q2–3.*
135. pretty] *Q1*; honest *Q2–3.*   148. cannot] *Q1*; can't *Q2–3.*
136. here] *Q1*; *om. Q2–3.*   151. tell] *Q1*; *om. Q2.*
141. go] *Q1*; do *Q2–3.*   154. full] *Q1*; *om. Q2–3.*

2 MOB.

Wauns, I'll have it. Captain, give me a shilling; I'll follow
you to the end of the world.

1 MOB.

Nay, dear Costar, duna; be advised.

PLUME.

Here, my hero, here are two guineas for thee as earnest of 160
what I'll do farther for thee.

1 MOB.

Duna take it, duna, dear Costar. *(Cries and pulls back his arm.)*

2 MOB.

I wull, I wull. Wauns, my mind gives me that I shall be a
captain myself. I take your money, sir, and now I'm a
gentlemen. 165

PLUME.

Give me thy hand. And now you and I will travel the world
o'er and command wherever we tread. *(Aside.)* Bring
your friend with you if you can.

2 MOB.

Well, Tummas, must we part?

1 MOB.

No, Costar, I cannot leave thee. Come, Captain *(crying)*, 170
I'll e'en go along too, and if you have two honester, simpler
lads in your company than we twa been—I'll say no more.

PLUME.

Here, my lad. *(Gives him money.)* Now your name.

1 MOB.

Thummas Appletree.

PLUME.

And yours? 175

2 MOB.

Costar Pearmain.

PLUME.

Born where?

1 MOB.

Both in Herefordshire.

164. I'm] *Q1*; I am *Q2–3*.   170. cannot] *Q1*; canno *Q2–3*.
167. command] *Q1*; command it   170. S.D. *crying*] *Q1*; om. *Q2–3*.
Q2–3.   172. than] *Q3*; that *Q1–2*.

–43–

PLUME.

> Very well. Courage, my lads. Now we will sing over the
> hills and far away.   180
> > Courage, boys, 'tis one to ten,
> > But we return all gentlemen, &c.   [*Exeunt.*]

ACT III

                              The marketplace.
                       [*Enter*] Plume *and* Worthy.

WORTHY.

> I cannot forbear admiring the equality of our two fortunes.
> We loved two ladies; they met us halfway, and just as we
> were upon the point of leaping into their arms, fortune drops
> into their laps, pride possesses their hearts, a maggot fills
> their heads, madness takes 'em by the tail; they snort, kick   5
> up their heels, and away they run.

PLUME.

> And leave us here to mourn upon the shore, a couple of
> poor, melancholy monsters. What shall we do?

WORTHY.

> I have a trick for mine, the letter, you know, and the
> fortune-teller.   10

PLUME.

> And I have a trick for mine.

WORTHY.

> What is't?

PLUME.

> I'll never think of her again.

WORTHY.

> No!

PLUME.

> No, I think myself above administering to the pride of any   15
> woman, were she worth twelve thousand a year, and I
> haven't the vanity to believe I shall even gain a lady worth
> twelve hundred. The generous, good-natured Silvia in her
> smock I admire, but the haughty, scornful Silvia with her
> fortune I despise.   20

179. we will] *Q1*; we'll *Q2–3*.

A SONG

1.

Come, fair one, be kind
You never shall find
A fellow so fit for a lover.
The world shall view
My passion for you,   25
But never your passion discover.

2.

I still will complain
Of your frowns and disdain,
Though I revel through all your charms.
The world shall declare   30
That I die with despair,
When I only die in your arms.

3.

I still will adore
And love more and more,
But, by Jove, if you chance to prove cruel,   35
I'll get me a miss
That freely will kiss,
Though I afterwards drink water gruel.

What, sneak out o'town and not so much as a word, a line,
a compliment! 'Sdeath, how far off does she live? I'd go   40
and break her windows.

WORTHY.

Ha, ha, ha. Ay, and the window bars too to come at her.
Come, come, friend, no more of your rough military airs.

Enter Kite.

KITE.

Captain, sir, look yonder; she's a-coming this way; 'tis the
prettiest, cleanest little tit.   45

PLUME.

Now, Worthy, to show you how much I'm in love. Here
she comes, and what is that great country fellow with her?

20.1–38. Song] *Q1*; *om. Q2–3*.   40. I'd] *Q1*; I'll *Q2–3*.
39. o'town] *Q1*; of town *Q2–3*.   46. I'm] *Q1*; I am *Q2–3*.

KITE.

    I can't tell, sir.

Enter Rose *and her brother* Bullock, Rose *with a basket on her arm crying chickens.*

ROSE.

    Buy chickens, young and tender; young and tender chickens.

PLUME.

    Here, you chickens.   50

ROSE.

    Who calls?

PLUME.

    Come hither, pretty maid.

ROSE.

    Will you please to buy, sir?

WORTHY.

    Yes, child, we'll both buy.

PLUME.

    Nay, Worthy, that's not fair; market for yourself. Come,   55
my child, I'll buy all you have.

ROSE.

    Then all I have is at your service.   *(Curtsies.)*

WORTHY.

    Then I must shift for myself, I find.   *Exit* [*Worthy*].

PLUME.

    Let me see. Young and tender, you say?

                                  (Chucks her under the chin.)

ROSE.

    As ever you tasted in your life, sir.   *(Curtsies.)* 60

PLUME.

    Come, I must examine your basket to the bottom, my dear.

ROSE.

    Nay, for that matter, put in your hand; feel, sir. I warrant
my ware as good as any in the market.

PLUME.

    And I'll buy it all, child, were it ten times more.

48.1–2. Rose *with . . . chickens*] *Q1*;   56. my] *Q1*; *om. Q2–3.*
and chickens on her arms in a basket,   57. S.D. *Curtsies*] *Q1*; *om. Q2–3.*
&c. Q2–3.

ROSE.

Sir, I can furnish you.   65

PLUME.

Come then; we won't quarrel about the price; they're fine
birds. Pray what's your name, pretty creature?

ROSE.

Rose, sir. My father is a farmer within three short mile o' th'
town. We keep this market; I sell chickens, eggs, and
butter, and my brother Bullock there sells corn.   70

BULLOCK.

Come, sister, hast ye; we shall be liate a whome.

(All this while Bullock *whistles about the stage.)*

PLUME.

Kite! *(He tips the wink upon* Kite, *who returns it.)*   Pretty
Mrs. Rose, you have, let me see, how many?

ROSE.

A dozen, sir, and they are richly worth a crown.

BULLOCK.

Come, Ruose, Ruose, I sold fifty stracke o'barley today in   75
half this time, but will you higgle and higgle for a penny
more than the commodity is worth.

ROSE.

What's that to you, oaf? I can make as much out of a groat
as you can out of fourpence, I'm sure. The gentleman bids
fair, and when I meet with a chapman, I know how to make   80
the best on him. And so, sir, I say for a crown piece the
bargain is yours.

PLUME.

Here's a guinea, my dear.

ROSE.

I can't change your money, sir.

71. hast] *Q1*; haste *Q2–3*.
71. liate a whome] *Q1*; lait hoame
Q2–3.
71.1. *All* ... Bullock] *Q1*; *om.*
Q2–3.

72. S.D. *He ... it*] *Q1*; *Tips him the*
wink; he returns it Q2–3.
75. o'barley] *Q1*; of barley *Q2–3*.
81. on] *Q1*; of *Q2–3*.
82. bargain is] *Q1*; bargain's *Q2–3*.

75. *stracke*] bushels.
80. *chapman*] a bargainer.

–47–

PLUME.

Indeed, indeed but you can. My lodging is hard by. You   85
shall bring home the chickens and we'll make change there.

[Plume] *goes off; she follows him.*

KITE.

So, sir, as I was telling you, I have seen one of these hussars
eat up a ravelin for his breakfast and afterwards pick his
teeth with a palisado.

BULLOCK.

Ay, you soldiers see very strange things. But pray, sir, what   90
is a ravelin?

KITE.

Why 'tis like a modern minced pie, but the crust is con-
founded hard and the plums are somewhat hard of digestion.

BULLOCK.

Then your palisado, pray what may he be?—Come, Ruose,
pray ha' done.   95

KITE.

Your palisado is a pretty sort of bodkin about the thickness
of my leg.

BULLOCK (*aside*).

That's a fib, I believe. Eh, where's Ruose? Ruose, Ruose,
'sflesh, where's Ruose gone?

KITE.

She's gone with the captain.   100

BULLOCK.

The captain! Wauns, there's no pressing of women, sure?

KITE.

But there is, sir.

BULLOCK.

If the captain should press Ruose, I should be ruined.
Which way went she? Oh, the devil take your rablins and
palisaders.   *Exit* [Bullock]. 105

85–86. by ... and] *Q1*; by,   105. palisaders] *Q1*; palisadoes
chicken, and *Q2–3*.   *Q2–3*.
88. pick] *Q1*; picked *Q2–3*.

---

88. *ravelin*] a fortification having two faces projecting outward from the
main structure to form an angle.
89. *palisado*] one of a row of large, pointed stakes set in the ground to
form a fence used for fortification.

KITE.

You shall be better acquainted with them, honest Bullock, or I shall miss of my aim.

Enter Worthy.

WORTHY.

Why thou'rt the most useful fellow in nature to your captain, admirable in your way, I find.

KITE.

Yes, sir, I understand my business, I will say it. You must 110 know, sir, I was born a gypsy and bred among that crew till I was ten year old. There I learned canting and lying. I was bought from my mother, Cleopatra, by a certain nobleman for three pistoles, who, liking my beauty, made me his page. There I learned impudence and pimping. I was turned off 115 for wearing my lord's linen and drinking my lady's brandy, and then turned bailiff's follower. There I learned bullying and swearing. I at last got into the army, and there I learned whoring and drinking. So that if your worship pleases to cast up the whole sum, *viz.*, canting, lying, impudence, 120 pimping, bullying, swearing, whoring, drinking, and a halberd, you will find the sum total will amount to a recruiting sergeant.

WORTHY.

And pray, what induced you to turn soldier?

KITE.

Hunger and ambition. The fears of starving and hopes of a 125 truncheon led me along to a gentleman with a fair tongue and fair periwig who loaded me with promises, but I gad 'twas the lightest load that I ever felt in my life. He promised to advance me, and indeed he did so, to a garret in the Savoy. I asked him why he put me in prison; he 130

108. thou'rt] *Q1*; thou art *Q2–3*.   *Q3.*
112. year] *Q1*; years *Q2–3*.   127–128. I gad 'twas] *Q1*; egad it
116. brandy] *Q1*; ratafia *Q2–3*.   was *Q2–3*.
122. will amount] *Q1–2*; amount   128. I ever] *Q1*; ever I *Q2–3*.

114. *pistoles*] either the Scottish twelve-pound piece of William III worth one English pound or a Spanish gold coin worth somewhat less.
122. *halberd*] combination spear and battle axe.
126. *truncheon*] a baton of authority.

called me lying dog and said I was in garrison, and indeed
'tis a garrison that may hold out till doomsday before I
should desire to take it again. But here comes Justice
Balance.

Enter Balance *and* Bullock.

BALANCE.

Here, you Sergeant, where's your captain? Here's a poor, 135
foolish fellow comes clamoring to me with a complaint that
your master has pressed his sister. Do you know anything of
this matter, Worthy?

WORTHY.

Ha, ha, ha. I know his sister is gone with Plume to his
lodgings to sell him some chickens.   140

BALANCE.

Is that all? The fellow's a fool.

BULLOCK.

I know that, an't please you, but if your worship pleases to
grant me a warrant to bring her before you for fear o' th'
worst.

BALANCE.

Thou art a mad fellow! Thy sister's safe enough.   145

KITE (*aside*).

I hope so too.

WORTHY.

Hast thou no more sense, fellow, than to believe that the
captain can list women?

BULLOCK.

I know not whether they list them, or what they do with
them, but I'm sure they carry as many women as men with 150
them out of the country.

BALANCE.

But how came you not to go along with your sister?

BULLOCK.

Luord, sir, I thought no more of her going than I do of the
day I shall die, but this gentleman, here, not suspecting any

---

142. an't] *Q1*; an *Q2-3*.   145. Thou . . . fellow] *Q1*; Thou'rt
143. o' th'] *Q1*; of the *Q2-3*.   mad, fellow *Q2-3*.

hurt neither, I believe. You thought no harm, friend, did 155
ye?

KITE.

Lack-a-day, sir, not I. (*Aside.*) Only that I believe I
shall marry her tomorrow.

BALANCE.

I begin to smell powder. Well, friend, but what did that
gentleman with you?   160

BULLOCK.

Why, sir, he entertained me with a fine story of a great fight
between the Hungarians, I think it was, and the Irish. And
so, sir, while we were in the heat of the battle, the captain
carried off the baggage.

BALANCE.

Sergeant, go along with this fellow to your captain. Give 165
him my humble service, and I desire him to discharge the
wench, though he has listed her.

BULLOCK.

Ay, and if he ben't free for that, he shall have another man
in her place.

KITE.

Come, honest friend. (*Aside.*) You shall go to my 170
quarters instead of the captain's.   *Exeunt* Kite *and* Bullock.

BALANCE.

We must get this mad captain his compliment of men and
send him a-packing, else he'll over-run the country.

WORTHY.

You see, sir, how little he values your daughter's disdain.

BALANCE.

I like him the better; I was much such another fellow at his 175
age. I never set my heart upon any woman so much as to
make me uneasy at the disappointment. But what was most
surprising both to myself and friends, I changed o' th'
sudden from the most fickle lover to be the most constant
husband in the world. But how goes your affair with 180
Melinda?

166. I] *Q1*; *om. Q2–3*.   177. me] *Q1*; myself *Q2–3*.
175. much] *Q1*; just *Q2–3*.   179. be] *Q1*; *om. Q2–3*.

WORTHY.

> Very slowly. Cupid had formerly wings, but I think in this
> age he goes upon crutches, or I fancy Venus had been
> dallying with her cripple Vulcan when my amour com-
> menced, which has made it go on so lamely. My mistress 185
> has got a captain too, but such a captain! As I live, yonder
> he comes.

BALANCE.

> Who? That bluff fellow in the sash? I don't know him.

WORTHY.

> But I engage he knows you, and everybody at first sight.
> His impudence were a prodigy were not his ignorance pro-   190
> portionable. He has the most universal acquaintance of
> any man living, for he won't be alone, and nobody will
> keep him company twice. Then he's a Caesar among the
> women: *veni, vidi, vici*, that's all. If he has but talked with
> the maid, he swears he has lain with the mistress, but the 195
> most surprising part of his character is his memory, which
> is the most prodigious and the most trifling in the world.

BALANCE.

> I have met with such men, and I take this good-for-nothing
> memory to proceed from a certain contexture of the brain,
> which is purely adapted to impertinencies, and they lodge 200
> secure, the owner having no thoughts of his own to disturb
> them. I have known a man as perfect as a chronologer as to
> the day and year of the most important transactions, but be
> altogether ignorant of the causes, springs, or consequences
> of any one thing of moment. I have known another acquire 205
> so much by travel as to tell you the names of most places in
> Europe, with their distances of miles, leagues, or hours as
> punctually as a post-boy, but for anything else, as ignorant
> as the horse that carries the mail.

WORTHY.

> This is your man, sir. Add but the traveler's privilege of 210
> lying, and even that he abuses. This is the picture, behold
> the life!

Enter Brazen.

183. had] has *Q1*; had been *Q2–3*.   204. springs] *Q1*; *om. Q2–3*.

-52-

BRAZEN.

Mr. Worthy, I'm your servant, and so forth. Heark'e, my dear.

WORTHY.

Whispering, sir, before company is not manners, and when 215 nobody's by, 'tis foolish.

BRAZEN.

Company! *Mort de ma vie*, I beg the gentleman's pardon. Who is he?

WORTHY.

Ask him.

BRAZEN.

So I will. My dear, I'm your servant, and so forth. Your 220 name, my dear?

BALANCE.

Very laconic, sir.

BRAZEN.

Laconic, a very good name truly. I have known several of the Laconics abroad. Poor Jack Laconic, he was killed at the battle of Landen. I remember that he had a blue ribband 225 in his hat that very day, and after he fell, we found a piece of neat's tongue in his pocket.

BALANCE.

Pray, sir, did the French attack us or we them at Landen?

BRAZEN.

The French attack us! Wauns, sir, are you a Jacobite?

BALANCE.

Why that question?   230

BRAZEN.

Because none but a Jacobite could think that the French durst attack us. No, sir, we attacked them on the—I have reason to remember the time, for I had two-and-twenty horses killed under me that day.

213. I'm] *Q1*; I am *Q2–3*.   220. I'm] *Q1*; I am *Q2–3*.

---

225. *Landen*] In 1693 William III was defeated at Landen, near Brussels, by the French.

227. *neat's*] cow's.

229. *Jacobite*] a supporter of the Stuart pretender, known to his adherents as James III.

WORTHY.

    Then, sir, you rid mighty hard.   235

BALANCE.

    Or perhaps, sir, like my countryman, you rid upon half a
dozen horses at once.

BRAZEN.

    What d'e mean, gentlemen. I tell you they were killed, all
torn to pieces by cannon shot, except six that I staked to
death upon the enemy's *chevaux de frise*.   240

BALANCE.

    Noble Captain, may I crave your name?

BRAZEN.

    Brazen, at your service.

BALANCE.

    Oh, Brazen, a very good name. I have known several of the
Brazens abroad.

WORTHY.

    Do you know Captain Plume, sir?   245

BRAZEN.

    Is he anything related to Frank Plume in Northampton-
shire? Honest Frank! Many, many a dry bottle have we
cracked hand to fist. You must have known his brother
Charles that was concerned in the India Company. He
married the daughter of old Tongue-Pad, the Master in 250
Chancery, a very pretty woman, only squinted a little. She
died in childbed of her first child, but the child survived.
'Twas a daughter, but whether 'twas called Margaret or
Marjory, upon my soul I can't remember. But, gentlemen
(*looking on his watch*), I must meet a lady, a twenty-thousand 255
pounder, presently, upon the walk by the water. Worthy,
your servant; Laconic, yours.   *Exit* [Brazen].

BALANCE.

    If you can have so mean an opinion of Melinda as to be
jealous of this fellow, I think she ought to give you cause to
be so.   260

235. rid] *Q1*; must have rid *Q2–3*.   239. that] *Q1*; *om. Q2–3*.
238. d'e] *Q1*; do you *Q2–3*.

---

240. *chevaux de frise*] a row of projecting spikes used to hinder enemy
horsemen.

WORTHY.

I don't think she encourages him so much for gaining herself a lover as to set me up a rival. Were there any credit to be given to his words, I should believe Melinda had made him this assignation. I must go see. Sir, you'll pardon me.   265

BALANCE.

Ay, ay, sir, you're a man of business.   [*Exit* Worthy].
But what have we got here?

Enter Rose *singing.*

ROSE.

And I shall be a lady, a captain's lady, and ride single upon a white horse with a star upon a velvet sidesaddle, and I shall go to London and see the tombs and the lions and the 270 Queen. Sir, an't please your worship, I have often seen your worship ride through our grounds a-hunting, begging your worship's pardon. Pray, what may this lace be worth a yard?   (*Showing some lace.*)

BALANCE.

Right Mechlin, by this light! Where did you get this lace, 275 child?

ROSE.

No matter for that, sir, I come honestly by't.

BALANCE.

I question it much.

ROSE.

And see here, sir, a fine turkey-shell snuff box, and fine mangeree, see here. (*She takes snuff affectedly.*) The 280 captain learnt me how to take it with an air.

BALANCE.

Oho, the captain! Now the murder's out. And so the captain taught you to take it with an air?

267.1. *Enter* Rose *singing*] *Q2–3*;   277. come] *Q1*; came *Q2–3*.
Enter Rose *singing what she pleases*   277. by't] *Q1*; by it *Q2–3*.
Q1.   280. S.D. *She takes*] *Q1*; *Takes*
271. an't] *Q1*; an *Q2–3*.   *Q2–3*.

275. *Mechlin*] a fine Belgian lace.
280. *mangeree*] Rose tries to remember orangeree, a popular brand of snuff flavored with the perfume of orange blossoms.

ROSE.

Yes, and give it with an air too. Will your worship please
to taste my snuff?   (*Offers the snuff affectedly.*) 285

BALANCE.

You're a very apt scholar, pretty maid, and pray what did
you give the captain for these fine things?

ROSE.

He's to have my brother for a soldier; and two or three
sweethearts that I have in the country, they shall all go with
the captain. Oh, he's the finest man and the humblest 290
withal. Would you believe it, sir, he carried me up with
him to his own chamber with as much gallantry as if I had
been the best lady in the land.

BALANCE.

Oh, he's a mighty familiar gentleman as can be.

ROSE.

But I must beg your worship's pardon. I must go seek out 295
my brother Bullock.   [Rose] *runs off singing.*

BALANCE.

If all officers took the same method of recruiting with this
gentleman, they might come in time to be fathers as well
as captains of their companies.

                    Enter Plume *singing.*
PLUME.

                    But it is not so   300
                    With those that go
                    Through frost and snow
                    Most apropo,
                    My maid with the milking pail.
                    (*Takes hold on* Rose, [*who has returned*].)
How, the justice! Then I'm arraigned, condemned, and 305
executed.

BALANCE.

Oh, my noble Captain.

ROSE.

And my noble captain too, sir.

PLUME.

'Sdeath, child, are you mad? Mr. Balance, I am so full of

286. You're] *Q1*; You are *Q2–3*.   295–299.] *Q1*; *om. Q2–3.*

business about my recruits that I ha'n't a moment's time   310
to—I have just now three or four people to—

BALANCE.

Nay, Captain, I must speak to you.

ROSE.

And so must I too, Captain.

PLUME.

Any other time, sir; I cannot for my life, sir—

BALANCE.

Pray, sir.   315

PLUME.

Twenty thousand things—I would but—now, sir, pray—
devil take me—I cannot—I must—   (*Breaks away.*)

BALANCE.

Nay, I'll follow you.   *Exit.*

ROSE.

And I too.   *Exit.*

[III.ii]   *The walk by the Severn side.*
                 Enter Melinda *and her maid* Lucy.

MELINDA.

And pray, was it a ring or buckle or pendants or knots, or
in what shape was the almighty gold transformed that has
bribed you so much in his favor?

LUCY.

Indeed, madam, the last bribe I had was from the captain,
and that was only a small piece of Flanders edging for   5
pinners.

MELINDA.

Ay, Flanders lace is as constant a present from officers to
their women as something else is from their women to them.
They every year bring over a cargo of lace to cheat the
Queen of her duty and her subjects of their honesty.   10

LUCY.

They only barter one sort of prohibited goods for another,
madam.

6. *pinners*] a caplike headdress.

MELINDA.

> Has any of them been bartering with you, Mrs. Pert,
> that you talk so like a trader?

LUCY.

> Madam, you talk as peevishly to me as if it were my fault.   15
> The crime is none of mine though I pretend to excuse it.
> Though he should not see you this week can I help it?
> But as I was saying, madam, his friend, Captain Plume, has
> so taken him up these two days—

MELINDA.

> Pshaw! Would his friend, the captain, were tied on his   20
> back. I warrant he has never been sober since that con-
> founded captain came to town. The devil take all officers,
> I say; they do the nation more harm by debauching us at
> home than they do good by defending us abroad. No sooner
> a captain comes to town, but all the young fellows flock   25
> about him, and we can't keep a man to ourselves.

LUCY.

> One would imagine, madam, by your concern for Worthy's
> absence, that you should use him better when he's with you.

MELINDA.

> Who told you, pray, that I was concerned for his absence?
> I'm only vexed that I've had nothing said to me these two   30
> days. One may like the love and despise the lover, I hope, as
> one may love the treason and hate the traitor. Oh, here
> comes another captain, and a rogue that has the confidence
> to make love to me; but indeed, I don't wonder at that
> when he has the assurance to fancy himself a gentleman.   35

LUCY (aside).

> If he should speak o' th' assignation, I should be ruined.

Enter Brazen.

BRAZEN.

> True to the touch, faith. (*Aside.*) I'll draw up all my
> compliments into one grand platoon and fire upon her at
> once.
>
> Thou peerless princess of Salopian plains,   40

---

13. them] *Q1*; 'em *Q2–3*.   20. on] *Q1*; upon *Q2–3*.
19. these] *Q1*; this *Q2–3*.   37–43.] *Q1*; *om. Q2–3*.

Envied by nymphs and worshipped by the swains,
Behold how humbly does the Severn glide,
To greet thee, princess of the Severn side.
Madam, I'm your humble servant and all that, madam. A
fine river this same Severn; do you love fishing, madam?   45

MELINDA.

'Tis a pretty melancholy amusement for lovers.

BRAZEN.

I'll go buy hooks and lines presently; for you must know,
madam, that I have served in Flanders against the French,
in Hungary against the Turks, and in Tangier against the
Moors, and I was never so much in love before. And split   50
me, madam, in all the campaigns I ever made I have not
seen so fine a woman as your ladyship.

MELINDA.

And from all the men I ever saw I never had so fine a
compliment, but you soldiers are the best-bred men, that we
must allow.   55

BRAZEN.

Some of us, madam, but there are brutes among us too, very
sad brutes. For my own part, I have always had the good
luck to prove agreeable. I have had very considerable offers,
madam. I might have married a German princess worth
fifty thousand crowns a year, but her stove disgusted me.   60
The daughter of a Turkish bashaw fell in love with me too,
when I was prisoner among the infidels. She offered to rob
her father of his treasure and make her escape with me, but
I don't know how, my time was not come. Hanging and
marriage, you know, go by destiny. Fate has reserved me   65
for a Shropshire lady with twenty thousand pound. Do
you know any such person, madam?

MELINDA.

Extravagant coxcomb! To be sure, a great many ladies
of that fortune would be proud of the name of Mrs. Brazen.

BRAZEN.

Nay, for that matter, madam, there are women of very   70
good quality of the name of Brazen.

44. I'm] *Q1*; I am *Q2-3.*

Enter Worthy.

MELINDA.

Oh, are you there, gentleman? Come, Captain, we'll walk
this way; give me your hand.

BRAZEN.

My hand, heart's blood, and guts are at your service.
Mr. Worthy, your servant, my dear. *Exit leading* Melinda.   75

WORTHY.

Death and fire! This is not to be borne.

Enter Plume.

PLUME.

No more it is, faith.

WORTHY.

What?

PLUME.

The March beer at the Raven. I have been doubly serving
the Queen, raising men and raising the excise. Recruiting   80
and elections are good friends to the excise.

WORTHY.

You an't drunk?

PLUME.

No, no, whimsical only; I could be mighty foolish and
fancy myself mighty witty. Reason still keeps its throne, but
it nods a little, that's all.   85

WORTHY.

Then you're just fit for a frolic.

PLUME.

As fit as close pinners for a punk in the pit.

WORTHY.

There's your play then; recover me that vessel from that
Tangerine.

PLUME.

She's well rigged, but how is she manned?   90

WORTHY.

By Captain Brazen that I told you of today. The frigate

72. gentleman] *Q1, Q3*; gentlemen   81. good] *Q1*; rare *Q2-3*.
Q2.   91. The frigate] *Q1*; she *Q2-3*.

87. *a punk in the pit*] a prostitute in the pit of the theater.

is called the Melinda, a first rate I can assure you. She
sheered off with him just now on purpose to affront me, but
according to your advice I would take no notice, because I
would seem to be above a concern for her behavior. But   95
have a care of a quarrel.

PLUME.

No, no, I never quarrel with anything in my cups but with
an oyster wench or a cook maid, and if they ben't civil, I
knock 'em down. But heark'e, my friend, I will make love,
and I must make love. I tell'e what, I'll make love like a   100
platoon.

WORTHY.

A platoon! How's that?

PLUME.

I'll kneel, stoop, and stand, faith. Most ladies are gained by
platooning.

WORTHY.

Here they come; I must leave you.   *Exit* [Worthy].   105

PLUME.

So, now I must look as sober and demure as a whore at a
christening.

Enter Brazen *and* Melinda.

BRAZEN.

Who's that, madam?

MELINDA.

A brother officer of yours, I suppose.

BRAZEN.

Ay! My dear.   (*To Plume.*)   110

PLUME.

My dear!   (*They run and embrace.*)

BRAZEN.

My dear boy, how is't? Your name, my dear. If I be not
mistaken, I have seen your face.

97–98. but with an] *Q1*; but an
Q2–3.
99. I will] *Q1*; I'll *Q2–3*.
100. tell'e] *Q1*; tell you *Q2–3*.
102. A platoon] *Q1*; Platoon
Q2–3.

106. I ... demure] *Q1*; must I
look as sober and as demure *Q2–3*.
109. suppose] *Q1*; suppose, sir
Q2–3.
111. S.D. *They ... embrace*] *Q1*;
Run and embrace Q2–3.

PLUME.

    I never see yours in my life, my dear. But there's a face well
    known as the sun's, that shines on all and is by all adored.   115

BRAZEN.

    Have you any pretensions, sir?

PLUME.

    Pretensions?

BRAZEN.

    That is, sir, have you ever served abroad?

PLUME.

    I have served at home, sir, for ages served this cruel fair.
    And that will serve the turn, sir.   120

MELINDA.

    So, between the fool and the rake I shall bring a fine spot
    of work upon my hands. (*Aside.*) I see Worthy yonder;
    I could be content to be friends with him would he come this
    way.

BRAZEN.

    Will you fight for the lady, sir?   125

PLUME.

    No, sir, but I'll have her notwithstanding.
        Thou peerless princess of Salopian plains,
        Envied by nymphs and worshipped by the swains.

BRAZEN.

    Wauns, sir, not fight for her!

PLUME.

    Prithee be quiet, I shall be out.   130
        Behold how humbly does the Severn glide
        To greet thee, princess of the Severn side.

BRAZEN.

    Don't mind him, madam. If he were not so well dressed, I
    should take him for a poet, but I'll show you the difference
    presently. Come, madam, we'll place you between us, and 135
    now the longest sword carries her.

                              (*Draws*, Melinda *shrieks.*)

                  Enter Worthy.

136.1. S.D.   *shrieks*] *Q1*; *shrieking*
Q2–3.

MELINDA.

> Oh, Mr. Worthy, save me from these madmen.
>
> > [Melinda] *runs off with* Worthy.

PLUME.

> Ha, ha, ha. Why don't you follow, sir, and fight the bold
> ravisher?

BRAZEN.

> No, sir, you're my man.   140

PLUME.

> I don't like the wages, and I won't be your man.

BRAZEN.

> Then you're not worth my sword.

PLUME.

> No, pray what did it cost?

BRAZEN.

> It cost my enemies thousands of lives, sir.

PLUME.

> Then they had a dear bargain.   145

> > *Enter* Silvia *dressed in man's apparel.*

SILVIA.

> Save ye, save ye, gentlemen.

BRAZEN.

> My dear, I'm yours.

PLUME.

> Do you know the gentleman?

BRAZEN.

> No, but I will presently. Your name, my dear?

SILVIA.

> Wilful, Jack Wilful at your service.   150

BRAZEN.

> What! The Kentish Wilfuls or those of Staffordshire?

SILVIA.

> Both sir, both; I'm related to all the Wilfuls in Europe, and
> I'm head of the family at present.

137.1. *runs off with*] *Q1*; *Exit with*   twenty pistoles in France, and my
Q2–3.   enemies thousands of lives in
140. you're] *Q1*; you are *Q2–3*.   Flanders *Q2–3*.
144. It ... sir] *Q1*; It cost me   145.1. *dressed*] *Q1*; *om. Q2–3*.

PLUME.

　　Do you live in the country, sir?

SILVIA.

　　Yes, sir, I live where I should. I have neither home, house,   155
　　nor habitation beyond this spot of ground.

BRAZEN.

　　What are you, sir?

SILVIA.

　　A rake.

PLUME.

　　In the army, I presume.

SILVIA.

　　No, but I intend to list immediately. Look'e, gentlemen,   160
　　he that bids me fairest shall have me.

BRAZEN.

　　Sir, I'll prefer you; I'll make you a corporal this minute.

PLUME.

　　A corporal! I'll make you my companion; you shall eat
　　with me.

BRAZEN.

　　You shall drink with me.   165

PLUME.

　　You shall lie with me, you young rogue.   (*Kisses her.*)

BRAZEN.

　　You shall receive your pay and do no duty.

SILVIA.

　　Then you must make me a field officer.

PLUME.

　　Pho, pho, I'll do more than all this. I'll make you a corporal
　　and give you a brevet for sergeant.   170

BRAZEN.

　　Can you read and write, sir?

SILVIA.

　　Yes.

154. the] *Q1*; this *Q2-3*.   162. prefer you] *Q1*, *Q3*; prefer
155. should] *Q1*; stand *Q2-3*.   your *Q2*.
160. I] *Q1*; *om. Q2-3*.   166. S.D. *her*] *Q1*; *om. Q2-3*.
161. shall have] *Q1*; has *Q2-3*.

BRAZEN.

Then your business is done. I'll make you chaplain to the
regiment.

SILVIA.

Your promises are so equal that I'm at a loss to choose. 175
There is one Plume that I hear much commended in town;
pray which of you is Captain Plume?

PLUME.

I'm Captain Plume.

BRAZEN.

No, no, I am Captain Plume.

SILVIA.

Hey day!   180

PLUME.

Captain Plume, I'm your servant, my dear.

BRAZEN.

Captain Brazen, I'm yours. The fellow dare not fight.

Enter Kite, *goes to whisper* Plume.

KITE.

Sir, if you please—

PLUME.

No, no, there's your captain. Captain Plume, your sergeant
here has got so drunk he mistakes me for you.   185

BRAZEN.

He's an incorrigible sot. Here, my Hector of Holbourn,
forty shillings for you.

PLUME.

I forbid the banns. Look'e, friend, you shall list with
Captain Brazen.

SILVIA.

I will see Captain Brazen hanged first. I will list with 190
Captain Plume. I'm a freeborn Englishman and will be a
slave my own way. Look'e, sir, will you stand by me?

(*To* Brazen.)

BRAZEN.

I warrant you, my lad.

178. I'm] *Q1*; I am *Q2–3*.   182. dare] *Q1–2*; dares *Q3*.
179. I am] *Q1*; I'm *Q2–3*.   185. here] *Q1*; *om. Q2–3*.
182. I'm] *Q1*; I am *Q2–3*.   191. I'm] *Q1*; I am *Q2–3*.

SILVIA.

    Then I will tell you, Captain Brazen (*to* Plume), that you
are an ignorant, pretending, impudent coxcomb.   195

BRAZEN.

    Ay, ay, a sad dog.

SILVIA.

    A very sad dog. Give me the money, noble Captain Plume.

PLUME.

    Hold, hold, then you won't list with Captain Brazen?

SILVIA.

    I won't.

BRAZEN.

    Never mind him, child. I'll end the dispute presently. 200
Heark'e, my dear.

    (*Takes* Plume *to one side of the stage and entertains him in dumb show.*)

KITE.

    Sir, he in the plain coat is Captain Plume; I'm his sergeant
and will take my oath on't.

SILVIA.

    What, are you Sergeant Kite?

KITE.

    At your service.   205

SILVIA.

    Then I would not take your oath for a farthing.

KITE.

    A very understanding youth of his age. Pray, sir, let me look
you full in the face.

SILVIA.

    Well, sir, what have you to say to my face?

KITE.

    The very image and superscription of my brother. Two 210
bullets of the same caliber were never so like. Sure it must
be Charles, Charles.

SILVIA.

    What d'ye mean by Charles?

198. Hold, hold] *Q1*; *om. Q2–3.*   210. and superscription] *Q1*; *om.*
202. I'm] *Q1*; I am *Q2–3.*   *Q2–3.*
208. the] *Q1–2*; your *Q3.*

KITE.

> The voice too, only a little variation in effa ut flat. My dear
> brother, for I must call you so, if you should have the 215
> fortune to enter into the most noble society of the sword, I
> bespeak you for a comrade.

SILVIA.

> No, sir, I'll be your captain's comrade if anybody's.

KITE.

> Ambition. There again, 'tis a noble passion for a soldier;
> by that I gained this glorious halberd. Ambition! I see a 220
> commission in his face already. Pray, noble Captain, give
> me leave to salute you.   (*Offers to kiss her.*)

SILVIA.

> What, men kiss one another!

KITE.

> We officers do; 'tis our way. We live together like man and
> wife, always either kissing or fighting. But I see a storm 225
> a-coming.

SILVIA.

> Now, Sergeant, I shall see who is your captain by your
> knocking down the t'other.

KITE.

> My captain scorns assistance, sir.

BRAZEN.

> How dare you contend for anything and not dare to draw 230
> your sword? But you're a young fellow and have not been
> much abroad; I excuse that, but prithee resign the man,
> prithee do. You're a very honest fellow.

PLUME.

> You lie, and you're a son of a whore.
>
>   (*Draws and makes up to* Brazen.)

BRAZEN (*retiring*).

> Hold, hold, did not you refuse to fight for the lady?   235

---

214. effa ut flat] C fa ut flat *Q1*;   231. you're] *Q1*; you are *Q2–3*.
Effa ut flatt *Q2–3*.   233. You're] *Q1*; You are *Q2–3*.
218. your] *Q1*; the *Q2–3*.   234. you're] *Q1*; you are *Q2–3*.

---

214. *effa ut flat*] the fuller name (F fa ut) of the note F, which was sung
to the syllable fa or ut according as it occurred in one or other of the
hexachords (imperfect scales) to which it could belong (*OED*, III, 47).

PLUME.

I always do, but for a man I'll fight knee deep, so you lie again.

(Plume *and* Brazen *fight.* Silvia *draws and is held by* Kite, *who takes* Silvia *in his arms and carries her off the stage.*)

BRAZEN.

Hold! Where's the man?

PLUME.

Gone.

BRAZEN.

Then what do we fight for? (*Puts up.*)   Now let's embrace, 240 my dear.

PLUME.

With all my heart, my dear. (*Puts up.*)   I suppose Kite has listed him by this time.   (*They embrace.*)

BRAZEN.

You're a brave fellow. I always fight with a man before I make him my friend, and if once I find he will fight, I 245 never quarrel with him afterwards. And now I'll tell you a secret, my dear friend. That lady that we frighted out o'the walk just now I found in bed this morning, so beautiful, so inviting. I presently locked the door. But I'm a man of honor. But I believe I shall marry her nevertheless; her 250 twenty thousand pound, you know, will be a pretty convenience. I had an assignation with her here, but your coming spoiled my sport, curse ye, my dear. But don't do so again.

PLUME.

No, no, my dear. Men are my business at present. *Exeunt.* 255

237.1–2. Plume ... *stage*] Plume and Brazen *fight a traverse or two about the stage.* Silvia *draws and is held by* Kite, *who sounds to arms with his mouth, takes* Silvia *in his arms, and carries her off the stage.* Q1; Plume and Brazen *fight a traverse or two about the stage.* Silvia *draws, who is held by* Kite, *who sounds to arms with his mouth, takes* Silvia *in his arms, and carries her off the stage.* Q2–3.

242. S.D. *puts*] Q1; *putting* Q2–3.
243. S.D. *They embrace*] Q1; *Embrace* Q2–3.
244. You're] Q1; You are Q2–3.
247. that] Q1; om. Q2–3.
247. o'the] Q1; of the Q2–3.
249. I'm] Q1; I am Q2–3.
253. ye] Q1; you Q2–3.

ACT IV

[IV.i]   *The walk by the Severn side.*
                          Enter Rose *and* Bullock *meeting.*

ROSE.

Where have you been, you great booby? You're always out
o'th' way in the time of preferment.

BULLOCK.

Preferment. Who should prefer me?

ROSE.

I would prefer you. Who should prefer a man but a woman?
Come throw away that great club, hold up your head, cock   5
your hat, and look big.

BULLOCK.

Ah, Ruose, Ruose, I fear somebody will look big sooner
than folk think of. This genteel breeding never comes into
the country without a train of followers. Here has been
Cartwheel, your sweetheart. What will become o' him?   10

ROSE.

Look'e, I'm a great woman and will provide for my rela-
tions. I told the captain how finely he could play upon the
tabor and pipe, so he has set him down for a drum major.

BULLOCK.

Nay, sister, why did not you keep that place for me? You
know I always loved to be a-drumming, if it were but on a   15
table or on a quart pot.

                          Enter Silvia.

SILVIA.

Had I but a commission in my pocket, I fancy my breeches
would become me as well as any ranting fellow of 'em all,
for I take a bold step, a rakish toss, a smart cock, and an
impudent air to be the principal ingredients in the com-   20
position of a captain. What's here? Rose, my nurse's
daughter. I'll go and practice. Come, child, kiss me at
once. (*Kisses* Rose.)   And her brother too. Well, honest

0.1. *The ... side*] *Scene of the walk*   2. o'th'] *Q1*; *of the Q2–3.*
continues Q1; *Scene the walk continues*   10. o' him] *Q1*; *of him Q2–3.*
Q2–3.   12. could play] *Q1*; *played Q2–3.*
1. You're] *Q1*; *you are Q2–3.*   13. a] *Q1*; *om. Q2–3.*

Dungfork, do you know the difference between a horse
cart and a cart horse, eh? 25

BULLOCK.

I presume that your worship is a captain by your clothes
and your courage.

SILVIA.

Suppose I were, would you be contented to list, friend?

ROSE.

No, no, though your worship be a handsome man, there be
others as fine as you. My brother is engaged to Captain 30
Plume.

SILVIA.

Plume! Do you know Captain Plume?

ROSE.

Yes, I do, and he knows me. He took the very ribbands out
of his shirtsleeves and put them into my shoes. See there. I
can assure that I can do anything with the captain. 35

BULLOCK.

That is, in a modest way, sir. Have a care what you say,
Ruose; don't shame your parentage.

ROSE.

Nay, for that matter I am not so simple as to say that I can
do anything with the captain but what I may do with
anybody else. 40

SILVIA.

So. And pray what do you expect from this captain, child?

ROSE.

I expect, sir, I expect, but he ordered me to tell nobody.
But suppose that he should promise to marry me?

SILVIA.

You should have a care, my dear. Men will promise
anything beforehand. 45

ROSE.

I know that, but he promised to marry me afterwards.

BULLOCK.

Wauns, Ruose, what have you said?

24–25. horse cart] *Q1–2*; horse and
cart *Q3*.
33. very] *Q1*; *om. Q2–3*.
34. them] *Q1*; 'em *Q2–3*.
35. assure] *Q1*; assure you *Q2–3*.

SILVIA.

Afterwards! After what?

ROSE.

After I had sold him my chickens. I hope there's no harm
in that, though there be an ugly song of chickens and   50
'sparagus.

Enter Plume.

PLUME.

What, Mr. Wilful, so close with my market woman!

SILVIA (*aside*).

I'll try if he loves her. —Close, sir, ay, and closer yet, sir.
Come, my pretty maid, you and I will withdraw a little.

PLUME.

No, no, friend, I han't done with her yet.   55

SILVIA.

Nor have I begun with her, so I have as good a right as you
have.

PLUME.

Thou art a bloody, impudent fellow. Let her go, I say.

SILVIA.

Do you let her go.

PLUME.

Entendez vous français, mon petit garçon?   60

SILVIA.

Oui.

PLUME.

*Si vous voulez donc vous enroller dans ma companie, la demoiselle
sera à vous.*

SILVIA.

Avez-vous couché avec elle?

PLUME.

Non.   65

SILVIA.

Assurement?

PLUME.

Ma foi.

50–51. though ... 'sparagus] *Q1*;   58–69. Let her ... *donc*] *Q1*; *om.*
om. Q2–3.   *Q2–3*; *see Appendix A for substituted
                                        lines.*

SILVIA.

C'est assez. Je serai votre soldat.

PLUME.

La prenez donc. I'll change a woman for a man at any time.

ROSE.

But I hope, Captain, you won't part with me. (*Cries.*) I   70
have heard before that you captains used to sell your men.

BULLOCK (*crying*).

Pray, Captain, don't send Ruose to the West Indies.

PLUME.

Ha, ha, ha, West Indies! No, no, my honest lad, give me
thy hand. Nor you nor she shall move a step farther than I
do. This gentleman is one of us and will be kind to you,   75
Mrs. Rose.

ROSE.

But will you be so kind to me, sir, as the captain would?

SILVIA.

I can't be altogether so kind to you. My circumstances are
not so good as the captain's, but I'll take care of you, upon
my word.   80

PLUME.

Ay, ay, we'll all take care of her. She shall live like a
princess, and her brother here shall be—what would you be?

BULLOCK.

Ah, sir, if you had not promised the place of drum major.

PLUME.

Ay, that is promised, but what think ye of barrack master?
You're a person of understanding, and barrack master you   85
shall be. But what's become of this same Cartwheel you told
me of, my dear?

ROSE.

We'll go fetch him. Come, brother barrack master. We
shall find you at home, noble Captain.

Exit Rose *and* Bullock.

PLUME.

Yes, yes. And now, sir, here are your forty shillings.   90

---

70. But . . . *Cries*] *Q1*; *om. Q2–3.*   83. Ah] *Q1*; Oh *Q2–3.*
71. used] use *Q1*; us'd *Q2–3.*   84. ye] *Q1*; you *Q2–3.*
71.1. S.D. *crying*] *Q1*; *om. Q2–3.*   85. You're] *Q1*; You are *Q2–3.*

SILVIA.

Captain Plume, I despise your listing money. If I do serve,
'tis purely for love, of that wench I mean, for you must
know that among my other sallies, I have spent the best
part of my fortune in search of a maid, and could never find
one hitherto. So you may be assured that I won't sell my   95
freedom under a less purchase than I did my estate. So
before I list I must be certified that this girl is a virgin.

PLUME.

Mr. Wilful, I can't tell how you can be certified in that
point till you try, but upon my honor she may be a vestal
for ought that I know to the contrary. I gained her heart, 100
indeed, by some trifling presents and promises, and know-
ing that the best security for a woman's soul is her body, I
would have made myself master of that too, had not the
jealousy of my impertinent landlady interposed.

SILVIA.

So you want only an opportunity for accomplishing your   105
designs upon her?

PLUME.

Not at all. I have already gained my ends, which were
only the drawing in one or two of her followers. The
women, you know, are the loadstones everywhere. Gain
the wives and you're caressed by the husbands; please the 110
mistresses and you are valued by their gallants; secure an
interest with the finest women at court and you procure the
favor of the greatest men. So, kiss the prettiest country
wenches and you are sure of listing the lustiest fellows.
Some people may call this artifice, but I term it stratagem, 115
since it is so main a part of the service. Besides, the fatigue of
recruiting is so intolerable that unless we could make
ourselves some pleasure amidst the pain, no mortal would
be able to bear it.

SILVIA.

Well, sir, I'm satisfied as to the point in debate. But now 120

95. that] *Q1*; *om. Q2–3.*   111. their] *Q1*; the *Q2–3.*
98. how] *Q1*; you how *Q2–3.*   116. fatigue] *Q2–3*; fatigues *Q1.*
110. you're] *Q1*; you are *Q2–3.*   120. I'm] *Q1*; I am *Q2–3.*
111. mistresses] *Q1*; mistress *Q2–3.*

let me beg you to lay aside your recruiting airs, put on the
man of honor, and tell me plainly what usage I must expect
when I'm under your command.

PLUME.

You must know in the first place, then, that I hate to have
gentlemen in my company, for they are always troublesome 125
and expensive, sometimes dangerous; and 'tis a constant
maxim among us that those who know the least obey the
best. Notwithstanding all this, I find something so agreeable
about you that engages me to court your company, and I
can't tell how it is, but I should be uneasy to see you under 130
the command of anybody else. Your usage will chiefly
depend upon your behavior. Only this you must expect,
that if you commit a small fault I will excuse it, if a great
one, I'll discharge you, for something tells me I shall not be
able to punish you.   135

SILVIA.

And something tells me that if you do discharge me 'twill
be the greatest punishment you will inflict, for were we this
moment to go upon the greatest dangers in your profession,
they would be less terrible to me than to stay behind you.
And now your hand. This lists me, and now you are my 140
captain.

PLUME.

Your friend. (*Kisses her.*) 'Sdeath, there's something in
this fellow that charms me.

SILVIA.

One favor I must beg. This affair will make some noise, and
I have some friends that would censure my conduct if I 145
threw myself into the circumstances of a private sentinel of
my own head. I must, therefore, take care to be impressed
by the Act of Parliament. You shall leave that to me.

PLUME.

What you please as to that. Will you lodge at my quarters
in the meantime? You shall have part of my bed.   150

SILVIA.

Oh, fie, lie with a common soldier! Would not you rather
lie with a common woman?

127. among] *Q1*; amongst *Q2–3*.   137. will] *Q1*; can *Q2–3*.

PLUME.

No, faith, I am not that rake that the world imagines. I have
got an air of freedom which people mistake for lewdness in
me as they mistake formality in others for religion. The 155
world is all a cheat, only I take mine which is undesigned
to be more excusable than theirs, which is hypocritical. I
hurt nobody but myself, but they abuse all mankind. Will
you lie with me?

SILVIA.

No, no, Captain, you forget Rose. She's to be my bedfellow, 160
you know.

PLUME.

I had forgot; pray be kind to her.   *Exeunt severally.*

Enter Melinda *and* Lucy.

MELINDA.

'Tis the greatest misfortune in nature for a woman to want
a confidante. We are so weak that we can do nothing without assistance, and then a secret racks us worse than the 165
colic. I'm at this minute so sick of a secret that I'm ready to
faint away. Help me, Lucy.

LUCY.

Bless me, madam, what's the matter?

MELINDA.

Vapors only. I begin to recover. If Silvia were in town, I
could heartily forgive her faults for the ease of discovering 170
my own.

LUCY.

You're thoughtful, madam. Am not I worthy to know the
cause?

MELINDA.

You're a servant, and a secret would make you saucy.

LUCY.

Not unless you should find fault without a cause, madam.   175

MELINDA.

Cause or no cause, I must not lose the pleasure of chiding

153. I am] *Q1*; I'm *Q2–3*.   166. I'm at] *Q1*; I am at *Q2–3*.
162.1] *Archer begins a new scene at*   174. You're] *Q1*; You are *Q2–3*.
this point.

when I please. Women must discharge their vapors some-
where, and before we get husbands, our servants must
expect to bear with 'em.

LUCY.

Then, madam, you had better raise me to a degree above 180
a servant. You know my family, and that five hundred
pound would set me upon the foot of a gentlewoman and
make me worthy the confidence of any lady in the land.
Besides, madam, 'twill extremely encourage me in the
great design that I now have in hand.   185

MELINDA.

I don't find that your design can be of any great advantage
to you. 'Twill please me, indeed, in the humor I have of
being revenged on the fool for his vanity of making love to
me, so I don't much care if I do promise you five hundred
pound the day of my marriage.   190

LUCY.

That is the way, madam, to make me diligent in the
vocation of a confidante, which I think is generally to
bring people together.

MELINDA.

Oh, Lucy, I can hold my secret no longer. You must know
that, hearing of the famous fortune-teller in town, I went 195
disguised to satisfy a curiosity which has cost me dear. That
fellow is certainly the devil or one of his bosom favorites;
he has told me the most surprising things of my past life.

LUCY.

Things past, madam, can hardly be reckoned surprising
because we know them already. Did he tell you anything 200
surprising that was to come?

MELINDA.

One thing very surprising; he said I should die a maid.

LUCY.

Die a maid! Come into the world for nothing! Dear
madam, if you should believe him, it might come to pass,
for the bare thought on't might kill one in four-and-twenty 205
hours. And did you ask him any questions about me?

185. that] *Q1; om. Q2–3.*   190. the day of my] *Q1;* upon my
                                      day of *Q 2–3.*

MELINDA.

You, why I passed for you.

LUCY.

So, 'tis I that am to die a maid. But the devil was a liar
from the beginning; he can't make me die a maid; I have
put it out of his power already.   210

MELINDA.

I do but jest. I would have passed for you and called myself
Lucy, but he presently told me my name, my quality, my
fortune, and gave me the whole history of my life. He told
me of a lover I had in this country and described Worthy
exactly, but in nothing so well as in his present indifference. 215
I fled to him for refuge here today. He never so much as
encouraged me in my fright, but coldly told me that he was
sorry for the accident because it might give the town cause
to censure my conduct, excused his not waiting on me
home, made me a careless bow, and walked off. 'Sdeath, I 220
could have stabbed him, or myself, 'twas the same thing.
Yonder he comes. I will so slave him.

LUCY.

Don't exasperate him. Consider what the fortune-teller
told you. Men are scarce, and as times go, it is not impossible for a woman to die a maid.   225

Enter Worthy.

MELINDA.

No matter.

WORTHY.

I find she's warmed. I must strike while the iron is hot.
—You have a great deal of courage, madam, to venture
into the walks where you were so late frighted.

MELINDA.

And you have a quantity of impudence to appear before 230
me, that you have so lately affronted.

WORTHY.

I had no design to affront you, nor appear before you
either, madam. I left you here because I had business in
another place, and came hither thinking to meet another
person.   235

222. slave] *Q1*; use *Q2–3*.   229. late] *Q1*; lately *Q2–3*.

MELINDA.

Since you find yourself disappointed, I hope you'll withdraw to another part of the walk.

WORTHY.

The walk is as free for me as you, madam, and broad enough
for us both.   (*They walk one by another.*)   Will you please to
take snuff, madam?   240

(*He offers her his box; she strikes it out of his hand. While he is gathering it
up, enter Brazen, who takes Melinda about the middle; she cuffs him.*)

BRAZEN.

What, here before me, my dear!

MELINDA.

What means this insolence?

LUCY (*runs to Brazen*).

Are you mad? Don't you see Mr. Worthy?

BRAZEN.

No, no, I'm struck blind. Worthy. Adso, well turned. My
mistress has wit at her finger's ends. Madam, I ask your   245
pardon; 'tis our way abroad. Mr. Worthy, you're the
happy man?

WORTHY.

I don't envy your happiness very much if the lady can
afford no other sort of favors but what she has bestowed
upon you.   250

MELINDA.

I'm sorry the favor miscarried, for it was designed for you,
Mr. Worthy, and be assured, 'tis the last and only favor you
must expect at my hands. Captain, I ask your pardon.

Exit with Lucy.

BRAZEN.

I grant it. You see, Mr. Worthy, 'twas only a random shot;
it might ha' taken off your head as well as mine. Courage,   255

---

238. as free . . . and] *Q1*; om. *Q2–3*.
239. S.D. *They . . . another*] *They
walk one by another, he with his hat
cocked, she fretting and tearing her fan.
Q1*; *They walk by one another . . . her
fan. Q2–3*.

240.2. *enter . . . middle*] *Q1*; *Brazen
takes her round the waist Q2–3*.
242.1. S.D. *runs to* Brazen] *Q1*; *to*
Brazen *Q2–3*.
246. you're] *Q1*; you are *Q2–3*.
251. I'm] *Q1*; I am *Q2–3*.
255. ha'] *Q1*; have *Q2–3*.

my dear, 'tis the fortune of war. But the enemy has thought
fit to withdraw, I think.

WORTHY.

Withdraw! Wauns, sir, what d'ye mean by withdraw?

BRAZEN.

I'll show you.   *Exit* [Brazen].

WORTHY.

She's lost, irrecoverably lost, and Plume's advice has 260
ruined me. 'Sdeath, why should I that knew her haughty
spirit be ruled by a man that is a stranger to her pride.

Enter Plume.

PLUME.

Ha, ha, ha, a battle royal. Don't frown so, man, she's
your own, I tell'e. I saw the fury of her love in the extremity
of her passion. The wildness of her anger is a certain sign 265
that she loves you to madness. That rogue, Kite, began the
battle with abundance of conduct and will bring you off
victorious, my life on't. He plays his part admirably; she's
to be with him again presently.

WORTHY.

But what could be the meaning of Brazen's familiarity with 270
her?

PLUME.

You are no logician if you pretend to draw consequences
from the actions of fools. There's no arguing by the rule of
reason upon a science without principles, and such is their
conduct. Whim, unaccountable whim hurries them on 275
like a man drunk with brandy before ten o'clock in the
morning. But we lost our sport; Kite has opened above an
hour ago. Let's away.   *Exeunt.*

[IV.ii]   *A chamber, a table with books and globes.*
          Kite, *disguised in a strange habit, and sitting at the table.*

KITE (*rising*).

By the position of the heavens, gained from my observation

262. that is] *Q1*; that's *Q2–3*.   275. them] *Q1*; 'em *Q2–3*.
264. tell'e] *Q1*; tell you *Q2–3*.

upon these celestial globes, I find that Luna was a tidewaiter, Sol a surveyor, Mercury a thief, Venus a whore,
Saturn an alderman, Jupiter a rake, and Mars a sergeant
of grenadiers. And this is the system of Kite the conjurer.   5

Enter Plume *and* Worthy.

PLUME.

Well, what success?

KITE.

I have sent away a shoemaker and a tailor already; one's
to be a captain of marines and the other a major of dragoons.
I am to manage them at night. Have you seen the lady,
Mr. Worthy?   10

WORTHY.

Ay, but it won't do. Have you showed her her name that I
tore off from the bottom of the letter?

KITE.

No, sir, I reserve that for the last stroke.

PLUME.

What letter?

WORTHY.

One that I would not let you see for fear you should break   15
Melinda's windows in good earnest.   (*Knocking at the door.*)

KITE.

Officers to your post.   *Exeunt* Worthy *and* Plume.
Tycho, mind the door.

(*Servant opens the door and enter a* Smith.)

SMITH.

Well, master, are you the cunning man?

KITE.

I am the learned Copernicus.   20

SMITH.

Well, Master Coppernose, I'm but a poor man and I can't
afford above a shilling for my fortune.

---

15. fear you] *Q1*; fear that you   18. *Tycho*] *Q1*; *om. Q2–3*.
Q2–3.   18.1. *and*] *Q1*; *om. Q1*.
16. Melinda's] *Q1*; *om. Q2–3*.   21. Coppernose] *Q1*; *om. Q2–3*.

2–3. *tidewaiter*] a customs official.
18. *Tycho*] The name of Kite's servant calls to mind the sixteenth-
century Danish astronomer, Tycho Brahe.

KITE.

Perhaps that is more than 'tis worth.

SMITH.

Look'e, Doctor, let me have something that's good for my
shilling, or I'll have my money again.   25

KITE.

If there be faith in the stars, you shall have your shilling
forty fold. Your hand, countryman. You are by trade a
smith.

SMITH.

How the devil should you know that?

KITE.

Because the devil and you are brother tradesmen. You   30
were born under Forceps.

SMITH.

Forceps, what's that?

KITE.

One of the signs. There's Leo, Sagitarius, Forceps, Furns,
Dixmude, Namur, Brussels, Charleroy, and so forth. Twelve
of 'em. Let me see. Did you ever make any bombs or   35
cannon's bullets?

SMITH.

Not I.

KITE.

You either have or will. The stars have decreed that you
shall be—I must have more money, sir, your fortune's
great.   40

SMITH.

Faith, Doctor, I have no more.

KITE.

Oh, sir, I'll trust you and take it out of your arrears.

SMITH.

Arrears! What arrears?

KITE.

The five hundred pound that's owing to you from the
government.   45

27. You are] *Q1*; You're *Q2–3*.

_____

31. *Forceps*] a smith's tongs.

SMITH.

Owing me!

KITE.

Owing you, sir. Let me see your t'other hand. I beg your pardon; it will be owing to you, and the rogue of an agent will demand fifty per cent for a fortnight's advance.

SMITH.

I'm in the clouds, Doctor, all this while.   50

KITE.

So am I, sir, among the stars. In two years, three months, and two hours, you will be made Captain of the Forges to the Grand Train of Artillery, and will have ten shillings a day and two servants. 'Tis the decree of the stars, and of the fixed stars, that are as immovable as your anvil. Strike,   55 sir, while the iron is hot. Fly, sir, be gone.

SMITH.

What would you have me do, Doctor? I wish the stars put me in a way for this fine place.

KITE.

The stars do. Let me see. Ay, about an hour hence walk carelessly into the market place and you'll see a tall, slender   60 gentleman cheapening a pen'worth of apples, with a cane hanging upon his button. This gentleman will ask you what's o'clock. He's your man and the maker of your fortune. Follow him, follow him. And now go home and take leave of your wife and children. An hour hence exactly   65 is your time.

SMITH.

A tall, slender gentleman, you say, with a cane. Pray, what sort of a head has the cane?

KITE.

An amber head with a black ribband.

SMITH.

But pray, of what employment is the gentleman?   70

---

51. So . . . sir,] *Q1*; Sir, I am above 'em *Q2–3*.
53. shillings] *Q1*; shilling *Q2–3*.

61. pen'worth] *Q1*; pennyworth *Q2–3*.
68. of a head] *Q1*; of head *Q2–3*.
70. But] *Q1*; And *Q2–3*.

KITE.

> Let me see. He's either a collector of the excise, a pleni-
> potentiary, or a captain of grenadiers. I can't tell exactly
> which. But he'll call you honest—Your name is?

SMITH.

> Thomas.

KITE.

> Right, he'll call you honest Tom.   75

SMITH.

> But how the devil should he know my name?

KITE.

> Oh, there are several sorts of Toms. Tom a Lincoln, Tom-tit,
> Tom Telltroth, Tom o' Bedlam, Tom Fool. (*Knocking at
> the door.*)   Be gone. An hour hence precisely.

SMITH.

> You say he'll ask me what's o'clock?   80

KITE.

> Most certainly, and you'll answer you don't know, but be
> sure to look at St. Mary's dial, for the sun won't shine, and
> if it should, you won't be able to tell the figures.

SMITH.

> I will, I will.   *Exit* [Smith].

PLUME (*behind*).

> Well done, conjurer, go on and prosper.   85

KITE.

> As you were.

Enter a Butcher.

KITE (*aside*).

> What, my old friend Pluck, the butcher. I offered the
> surly bulldog five guineas this morning and he refused it.

BUTCHER.

> So, Master Conjurer, here's half a crown. And now you
> must understand—   90

KITE.

> Hold, friend, I know your business beforehand.

BUTCHER.

> You're devilish cunning then, for I don't well know it
> myself.

71. excise, a] *Q1*; excise, or a *Q2–3*.   75. Right] *Q1*; *om. Q2–3.*

KITE.

> I know more than you, friend. You have a foolish saying
> that such a one knows no more than the man in the moon.   95
> I tell you the man in the moon knows more than all the
> men under the sun; don't the moon see all the world?

BUTCHER.

> All the world see the moon, I must confess.

KITE.

> Then she must see all the world, that's certain. Give me your
> hand. You are by trade either a butcher or a surgeon.   100

BUTCHER.

> True, I am a butcher.

KITE.

> And a surgeon you will be.   The employments differ only
> in the name. He that can cut up an ox may dissect a man,
> and the same dexterity that cracks a marrow bone will cut
> off a leg or an arm.   105

BUTCHER.

> What d'ye mean, Doctor, what d'ye mean?

KITE.

> Patience, patience, Mr. Surgeon General. The stars are
> great bodies and move slowly.

BUTCHER.

> But what d'ye mean by Surgeon General, Doctor?

KITE.

> Nay, sir, if your worship won't have patience, I must beg   110
> the favor of your worship's absence.

BUTCHER.

> My worship, my worship! But why my worship?

KITE.

> Nay, then I have done.   (*Sits.*)

BUTCHER.

> Pray, Doctor.

KITE.

> Fire and fury, sir.   (*Rises in a passion.*)   Do you think the   115
> stars will be hurried? Do the stars owe you any money, sir,
> that you dare to dun their lordships at this rate? Sir, I am

100. You are] *Q1*; You're *Q2–3*.

porter to the stars, and I am ordered to let no dun come near
their doors.

BUTCHER.

Dear Doctor, I never had any dealings with the stars; they 120
don't owe me a penny. But since you are the porter, please
to accept of this half crown to drink their healths, and
don't be angry.

KITE.

Let me see your hand then, once more. Here has been gold,
five guineas, my friend, in this very hand this morning.   125

BUTCHER.

Nay, then he is the devil. Pray, Doctor, were you born of
a woman or did you come into the world of your own head?

KITE.

That's a secret. This gold was offered you by a proper,
handsome man called Hawk or Buzzard or—

BUTCHER.

Kite, you mean.   130

KITE.

Ay, ay, Kite.

BUTCHER.

As errant a rogue as ever carried a halberd. The impudent
rascal would have decoyed me for a soldier.

KITE.

A soldier! A man of your substance for a soldier! Your
mother has a hundred pound in hard money lying at this 135
minute in the hands of a mercer, not forty yards from this
place.

BUTCHER.

Wauns, and so she has, but very few know so much.

KITE.

I know it, and that rogue, what's his name, Kite, knew it,
and offered you five guineas to list because he knew your 140
poor mother would give the hundred for your discharge.

BUTCHER.

There's a dog now. 'Flesh, Doctor, I'll give you t'other

120. dealings] *Q1*; dealing *Q2–3*.   135. a hundred] *Q1*; an hundred
121. the] *Q1*; their *Q2–3*.   *Q2–3*.
                                                     142. 'Flesh] *Q1*; 'Sflesh *Q2–3*.

half crown, and tell me that this same Kite will be hanged.

KITE.

He's in as much danger as any man in the county of Salop.

BUTCHER.

There's your fee, but you have forgot the Surgeon General 145
all this while.

KITE.

You put the stars in a passion. (*Looks on his books.*) But
now they're pacified again. Let me see. Did you never cut
off a man's leg?

BUTCHER.

No.   150

KITE.

Recollect, pray.

BUTCHER.

I say no.

KITE.

That's strange, wonderful strange, but nothing is strange
to me, such wonderful changes have I seen. The second or
third, ay, the third campaign that you make in Flanders, the 155
leg of a great officer will be shattered by a great shot. You
will be there accidentally and with your cleaver chop off
the limb at a blow. In short, the operation will be performed
with so much dexterity that with the general applause you
will be made Surgeon General of the whole army.   160

BUTCHER.

Nay, for the matter of cutting off a limb, I'll do't. I'll do't
with any surgeon in Europe, but I have no thoughts of
making a campaign.

KITE.

You have no thoughts! What matter for your thoughts?
The stars have decreed it, and you must go.   165

BUTCHER.

The stars decree it. Wauns, sir, the justices can't press me.

KITE.

Nay, friend, 'tis none of my business; I ha' done. Only

148. they're] *Q1*; they are *Q2–3*.   164. What] *Q1*; What's *Q2–3*.
159. with the general] *Q1*; with   166. can't] *Q1, Q3*; can *Q2*.
general *Q2–3*.   167. ha'] *Q1*; have *Q2–3*.

mind this, you'll know more an hour and a half hence.
That's all. Farewell.   (*Going.*)

BUTCHER.

Hold, hold, Doctor, Surgeon General! Pray, what is the   170
place worth, pray?

KITE.

Five hundred pound a year, beside guineas for claps.

BUTCHER.

Five hundred pound a year! An hour and half hence you
say?

KITE.

Prithee, friend, be quiet, don't be so troublesome. Here's   175
such a work to make a booby butcher accept of five hundred
pound a year. But if you must hear it, I tell you in short,
you'll be standing in your stall an hour and half hence, and
a gentleman will come by with a snuff box in his hand and
the tip of his handkerchief hanging out of his right pocket. 180
He'll ask you the price of a loin of veal, and at the same
time stroke your great dog upon the head and call him
Chopper.

BUTCHER.

Mercy upon us; Chopper is the dog's name.

KITE.

Look'e there; what I say is true. Things that are to come   185
must come to pass. Get you home; sell off your stock. Don't
mind the whining and the sniveling of your mother and
your sister; women always hinder preferment. Make what
money you can and follow that gentleman. His name
begins with a P. Mind that. There will be the barber's   190
daughter, too, that you promised marriage to; she will be
pulling and hauling you to pieces.

BUTCHER.

What, know Sally too! He's the devil, and he needs must
go that the devil drives. (*Going.*) The tips of his handkerchief out of his left pocket?   195

171. Pray] *Q1*; *om. Q2–3.*   177. I . . . short] *Q1*; I tell in short
172, 173. pound] *Q1*; pounds *Q2–3.*   *Q2*; I'll tell you in short *Q3.*
173. and half] *Q1*; an a half *Q2–3.*   181. loin] *Q1*, *Q3*; line *Q2.*
                                        184. upon] *Q1–2*; on *Q3.*

KITE.

No, no, his right pocket. If it be the left, 'tis none of the man.

BUTCHER.

Well, well, I'll mind him.

PLUME (*behind with his pocket book*).

The right pocket, you say?

KITE.

I hear the rustling of silks. (*Knocking.*) Fly, sir, 'tis 200 Madam Melinda.

Enter Melinda *and* Lucy.

KITE.

Tycho, chairs for the ladies.

MELINDA.

Don't trouble yourself. We shan't stay, Doctor.

KITE.

Your ladyship is to stay much longer than you imagine.

MELINDA.

For what? 205

KITE.

For a husband. (*To* Lucy.) For your part, madam, you won't stay for a husband.

LUCY.

Pray, Doctor, do you converse with the stars or with the devil?

KITE.

With both. When I have the destinies of men in search, I 210 consult the stars; when the affairs of women come under my hand, I advise with my t'other friend.

MELINDA.

And have you raised the devil upon my account?

KITE.

Yes, madam, and he's now under the table.

LUCY.

Oh, heavens protect us! Dear madam, let us be gone. 215

208. or with the] *Q1*; or the *Q2–3*. 215. let us] *Q1*; let's *Q2–3*.
212. hand] *Q1*; hands *Q2–3*.

KITE.

If you be afraid of him, why do you come to consult him?

MELINDA.

Don't fear, fool. Do you think, sir, that because I'm a woman I'm to be fooled out of my reason or frighted out of my senses? Come, show me this devil.

KITE.

He's a little busy at present, but when he has done he shall 220 wait on you.

MELINDA.

What is he doing?

KITE.

Writing your name in his pocket book.

MELINDA.

Ha, ha, ha, my name! Pray, what have you or he to do with my name? 225

KITE.

Look'e, fair lady, the devil is a very modest person. He seeks nobody unless they seek him first. He's chained up like a mastiff and cannot stir unless he be let loose. You come to me to have your fortune told. Do you think, madam, that I can answer you of my own head? No, 230 madam, the affairs of women are so irregular that nothing less than the devil can give any account of 'em. Now to convince you of your incredulity, I'll show you a trial of my skill. Here, you, *Caco-demon del fuego*, exert your power. Draw me this lady's name, the word Melinda in the proper 235 letters and character of her own handwriting. Do it at three motions: one, two, three. 'Tis done. Now, madam, will you please to send your maid to fetch it.

LUCY.

I fetch it! The devil fetch me if I do.

217–218. I'm a woman] *Q1*; I am a woman *Q2–3*.
224. Ha, ha, ha] *Q1*; Ha, ha *Q2–3*.
232. 'em] *Q1*; them *Q2–3*.

234. *Caco-demon del fuego*] *Q1*; *Caco-demo del Plumo Q2–3*.
235–236. in ... character] *Q1*; in proper letters and characters *Q2–3*.

234. *Caco-demon del fuego*] demon from hell.

MELINDA.

My name in my own handwriting; that would be convincing 240
indeed.

KITE.

Seeing's believing. (*Goes to the table, lifts up the carpet.*)
Here Tre, Tre, poor Tre, give me the bone, sirrah.

(*He puts his hand under the table.* Plume *steals to the other side of the table
and catches him by the hand.*)

Oh, oh, the devil, the devil in good earnest. My hand, my
hand, the devil, my hand!   245

(Melinda *and* Lucy *shriek and run to a corner of the stage.* Kite *discovers*
Plume *and gets away his hand.*)

A plague o' your pincers; he has fixed his nails in my very
flesh. Oh, madam, you put the demon into such a passion
with your scruples that it has almost cost me my hand.

MELINDA.

It has cost us our lives almost. But have you got the name?

KITE.

Got it, ay, madam, I have got it here. I'm sure the blood 250
comes. But there's your name upon that square piece of
paper. Behold.

MELINDA.

'Tis wonderful. My very letters to a tittle.

LUCY.

'Tis like your hand, madam, but not so like your hand
neither; and now I look nearer, 'tis not like your hand 255
at all.

KITE.

Here's a chambermaid now that will out-lie the devil.

LUCY.

Look'e, madam, they shan't impose upon us. People can't
remember their hands no more than they can their faces.
Come, madam, let us be certain; write your name upon 260
this paper. (*Takes out paper and folds it.*)   Then we'll
compare the two names.

243.1–251. *He* . . . comes] *Q1*; *om.*   257. that] *Q1*; *om. Q2–3.*
Q2–3.

242. S.D. *carpet*] tablecloth.

KITE.

Anything for your satisfaction, madam. Here's pen and
ink.   (Melinda *writes and* Lucy *holds the paper.*)

LUCY.

Let me see it, madam. 'Tis the same, the very same. 265
(*Aside.*) But I'll secure one copy for my own affairs.

MELINDA.

This is demonstration.

KITE.

'Tis so, madam. The word demonstration comes from
demon, the father of lies.

MELINDA.

Well, Doctor, I'm convinced, and now pray what account 270
can you give me of my future fortune?

KITE.

Before the sun has made one course round this earthly
globe, your fortune will be fixed for happiness or misery.

MELINDA.

What, so near the crisis of my fate!

KITE.

Let me see. About the hour of ten tomorrow you will be 275
saluted by a gentleman who will come to take his leave
of you, being designed for travel. His intention of going
abroad is sudden, and the occasion a woman. Your fortune
and his are like the bullet and the barrel; one runs plump
into t'other. In short, if the gentleman travels, he will die 280
abroad; and if he does, you will die before he comes home.

MELINDA.

What sort of man is he?

KITE.

Madam, he is a fine gentleman and a lover, that is, a man
of very good sense and a very great fool.

MELINDA.

How is that possible, Doctor?   285

KITE.

Because, madam, because it is so. A woman's reason is
the best for a man's being a fool.

264. S.D. *writes and* Lucy] *Q1; writes,*   280. t'other] *Q1;* the other *Q2–3.*
Lucy *Q2–3.*   283. he is] *Q1;* he's *Q2–3.*
270. I'm] *Q1;* I am *Q2–3.*

MELINDA.

Ten o'clock, you say?

KITE.

Ten, about the hour of tea drinking throughout the
kingdom.　　　　　　　　　　　　　　　　　　　290

MELINDA.

Here, Doctor. (*Gives him money.*)　Lucy, have you any
questions to ask?

LUCY.

Oh, madam, a thousand.

KITE.

I must beg your patience till another time, for I expect
more company this minute; besides, I must discharge the　295
gentleman under the table.

LUCY.

Pray, sir, discharge us first.

KITE.

Tycho, wait on the ladies downstairs.　　*Exit* Melinda *and* Lucy.

Enter Plume *and* Worthy *laughing.*

KITE.

Ay, you may well laugh, gentlemen. Not all the cannon of
the French army could have frighted me so much as that　300
grip you gave me under the table.

PLUME.

I think, Mr. Doctor, I out-conjured you that bout.

KITE.

I was surprised, for I should not have taken a captain for a
conjurer.

PLUME.

No more than I should a sergeant for a wit.　　　　　305

KITE.

Mr. Worthy, you were pleased to wish me joy today; I
hope to be able to return the compliment tomorrow.

WORTHY.

I'll make it the best compliment to you that you ever made
in your life if you do, but I must be a traveler, you say?

291. S.D. *him*] *Q1*; *om. Q2–3*.　　　299–305.] *Q1*; *om. Q2–3*.
297. Pray] *Q1*; Oh, pray *Q2–3*.　　308–309. you . . . your] *Q1*; ever I
298.1. *laughing*] *Q1*; *om. Q2–3*.　　made in my *Q2–3*.

–92–

KITE.

No farther than the chops of the Channel, I presume, sir.   310

PLUME.

That we have concerted already.   (*Knocking hard.*)   Hey day. You don't profess midwifery, Doctor?

KITE.

Away to your ambuscade.   *Exeunt* Plume *and* Worthy.

Enter Brazen.

BRAZEN.

Your servant, servant, my dear.

KITE.

Stand off. I have my familiar already.   315

BRAZEN.

Are you bewitched, my dear?

KITE.

Yes, my dear, but mine is a peaceable spirit and hates gunpowder. Thus I fortify myself. (*Draws a circle round him.*) And now, Captain, have a care how you force my lines.   320

BRAZEN.

Lines! What dost talk of lines? You have something like a fishing rod there, indeed, but I come to be acquainted with you, man. What's your name, my dear?

KITE.

Conundrum.

BRAZEN.

Conundrum. Rat me, I know a famous doctor in London 325 of your name. Where were you born?

KITE.

I was born in Algebra.

BRAZEN.

Algebra! 'Tis no country in Christendom I'm sure, unless it be some pitiful place in the Highlands of Scotland.

KITE.

Right, I told you I was bewitched.   330

325. know] *Q1*; knew *Q2–3*.   329. pitiful] *Q1*; *om. Q2–3*.

310. *chops of the Channel*] the entrance to the English Channel from the Atlantic.

-93-

BRAZEN.

So am I, my dear. I'm going to be married. I've had two letters from a lady of fortune that loves me to madness, fits, colic, spleen, and vapors. Shall I marry her in four and twenty hours, ay or no?

KITE.

I must have the year and day o'th' month when these 335 letters were dated.

BRAZEN.

Why you old bitch, did you ever hear of love letters dated with the year and day o'th' month? Do you think *billets doux* are like bank bills?

KITE.

They are not so good. But if they bear no date, I must 340 examine the contents.

BRAZEN.

Contents, that you shall, old boy; here they be both.

KITE.

Only the last you received, if you please. (*Takes the letter.*)   Now, sir, if you please to let me consult my books for a minute, I'll send this letter enclosed to you with the 345 determination of the stars upon it to your lodgings.

BRAZEN.

With all my heart. I must give him— (*Puts his hand in's pocket.*)   Algebra! I fancy, Doctor, 'tis hard to calculate the place of your nativity. Here. (*Gives him money.*)   And if I succeed, I'll build a watchtower upon the top of the highest 350 mountain in Wales for the study of astrology and the benefit of Conundrums.   *Exit* [Brazen].

Enter Plume *and* Worthy.

WORTHY.

Oh, Doctor, that letter's worth a million. Let me see it. And now I have it, I'm afraid to open it.

PLUME.

Pho, let me see it. (*Opening the letter.*)   If she be a jilt, 355

331. I'm] *Q1*; I am *Q2-3*.   347. S.D. *in's*] *Q1*; *in his Q2-3*.
331. I've] *Q1*; I have *Q2-3*.   354. I'm] *Q1, Q3*; I am *Q2*.
335, 338. o'th'] *Q1*; of the *Q2-3*.

-94-

damn her, she is one. There's her name at the bottom on't.

WORTHY.

How! Then I will travel in good earnest. By all my hopes, 'tis Lucy's hand!

PLUME.

Lucy's!

WORTHY.

Certainly; 'tis no more like Melinda's character than 360 black is to white.

PLUME.

Then 'tis certainly Lucy's contrivance to draw in Brazen for a husband. But are you sure 'tis not Melinda's hand?

WORTHY.

You shall see. Where's the bit of paper I gave you just now that the devil writ Melinda upon? 365

KITE.

Here, sir.

PLUME.

'Tis plain; they're not the same. And is this the malicious name that was subscribed to the letter which made Mr. Balance send his daughter into the country?

WORTHY.

The very same. The other fragments I showed you just 370 now. I once intended it for another use, but I think I have turned it now to better advantage.

PLUME.

But 'twas barbarous to conceal this so long and to continue me so many hours in the pernicious heresy of believing that angelic creature could change. Poor Silvia! 375

WORTHY.

Rich Silvia, you mean, and poor Captain. Ha, ha, ha. Come, come, friend, Melinda is true and shall be mine. Silvia is constant and may be yours.

PLUME.

No, she's above my hopes, but for her sake, I'll recant my opinion of her sex. 380

357. I will] *Q1*; I'll *Q2–3*. 371–372. I once ... advantage]
365. writ] *Q1*; write *Q1–3*. *Q1*; *om. Q2–3*.

By some the sex is blam'd without design,
Light, harmless censure such as yours or mine,
Sallies of wit and vapors of our wine.
Others the justice of the sex condemn,
And wanting merit to create esteem,   385
Would hide their own defects by cens'ring them.
But they, secure in their all-conqu'ring charms,
Laugh at the vain efforts of false alarms;
He magnifies their conquests who complains,
For none would struggle were they not in chains.   390

[*Exeunt*].

ACT V

[V.i] *An antechamber, with a periwig, hat, and sword upon the table.*
Enter Silvia *in her nightcap.*

SILVIA.

I have rested but indifferently, and I believe my bedfellow
was as little pleased. Poor Rose. Here she comes.

Enter Rose.

Good morrow, my dear, how d'ye this morning?

ROSE.

Just as I was last night, neither better nor worse for you.

SILVIA.

What's the matter? Did you not like your bedfellow?   5

ROSE.

I don't know whether I had a bedfellow or not.

SILVIA.

Did not I lie with you?

ROSE.

No. I wonder you could have the conscience to ruin a poor
girl for nothing.

SILVIA.

I have saved thee from ruin, child. Don't be melancholy.   10
I can give you as many fine things as the captain can.

V.i] *This scene is entirely omitted in*
Q 2–3.

ROSE.

> But you can't, I'm sure.   (*Knocking at the door.*)

SILVIA.

> Odso, my accoutrements. (*Puts on her periwig, hat, and
> sword.*)   Who's at the door?

WITHOUT.

> Open the door or we'll break it down.   15

SILVIA.

> Patience a little.   (*Opens the door.*)

Enter Constable *and mob.*

CONSTABLE.

> We have 'em, we have 'em, the duck and the mallard both
> in the decoy.

SILVIA.

> What means this plot? Stand off. (*Draws.*)   The man
> dies that comes within reach of my point.   20

CONSTABLE.

> That is not the point, master. Put up your sword or I
> shall knock you down, and so I command the Queen's
> peace.

SILVIA.

> You are some blockhead of a constable?

CONSTABLE.

> I am so, and have a warrant to apprehend the bodies of you   25
> and your whore there.

ROSE.

> Whore! Never was poor woman so abused.

Enter Bullock *unbuttoned.*

BULLOCK.

> What's matter now? Oh, Mr. Bridewell, what brings you
> abroad so early?

CONSTABLE.

> This, sir. (*Lays hold of* Bullock.)   You're the Queen's   30
> prisoner.

BULLOCK.

> Wauns, you lie, sir; I'm the Queen's soldier.

CONSTABLE.

> No matter for that. You shall go before Justice Balance.

SILVIA.

    Balance, 'tis what I wanted. Here, Mr. Constable, I resign
    my sword.   35

ROSE.

    Can't you carry us before the captain, Mr. Bridewell?

CONSTABLE.

    Captain! Ha'n't you got your belly full of captains yet?
    Come, come, make way there.   *Exeunt.*

[V.ii]   Justice Balance's *house.*
                     [*Enter*] Balance *and* Scale.

SCALE.

    I say 'tis not to be borne, Mr. Balance.

BALANCE.

    Look'e, Mr. Scale, for my own part I shall be very tender in
    what regards the officers of the army. They expose their
    lives to so many dangers for us abroad that we may give
    them some grains of allowance at home.   5

SCALE.

    Allowance! This poor girl's father is my tenant, and if I
    mistake not, her mother nursed a child for you. Shall they
    debauch our daughters to our faces?

BALANCE.

    Consider, Mr. Scale, that were it not for the bravery of
    these officers we should have French dragoons among us   10
    that would leave us neither liberty, property, wife, nor
    daughter. Come, Mr. Scale, the gentlemen are vigorous
    and warm, and may they continue so. The same heat that
    stirs them up to love spurs them on to battle. You never
    knew a great general in your life that did not love a whore.   15
    This I only speak in reference to Captain Plume, for the
    other spark I know nothing of.

SCALE.

    Nor can I hear of anybody that does. Oh, here they come.

    Enter Silvia, Bullock, Rose (*prisoners*), Constable *and mob.*

---

5. grains] *Q1, Q3*; grain *Q2*.   11–12. wife, nor daughter] *Q1*;
                                                wives nor daughters *Q2–3*.

CONSTABLE.

    May it please your worships, we took them in the very act,
re infecta, sir. The gentleman indeed behaved like a gentle-   20
man, for he drew his sword and swore, and afterwards laid
it down and said nothing.

BALANCE.

    Give the gentleman his sword again. Wait you without.

                                     Exit Constable [*and mob*].

    (*To* Silvia.)   I'm sorry, sir, to know a gentleman upon such
terms that the occasion of our meeting should prevent the   25
satisfaction of an acquaintance.

SILVIA.

    Sir, you need make no apology for your warrant, nor more
than I shall do for my behavior. My innocence is upon an
equal foot with your authority.

SCALE.

    Innocence! Have you not seduced that young maid?   30

SILVIA.

    No, Mr. Goosecap, she seduced me.

BULLOCK.

    So she did, I'll swear, for she proposed marriage first.

BALANCE.

    What, then you're married, child?   (*To* Rose.)

ROSE.

    Yes, sir, to my sorrow.

BALANCE.

    Who was the witness?   35

BULLOCK.

    That was I. I danced, threw the stocking, and spoke jokes
by their bedside, I'm sure.

BALANCE.

    Who was the minister?

BULLOCK.

    Minister! We are soldiers and want no ministers. They
were married by the Articles of War.   40

23.1. *Exit ... mob*] *Exit constable,*   30. you not] *Q1*; not you *Q2–3*.
&c. Q1; *Exit constable and watch*   33. you're] *Q1*; you are *Q2–3*.
Q2–3.   39. ministers] *Q1*; minister *Q2–3*.

---

   20. *re infecta*] the act not having been accomplished.

BALANCE.

Hold thy prating, fool. Your appearance, sir, promises
some understanding. Pray, what does this fellow mean?

SILVIA.

He means marriage, I think, but that, you know, is so odd a
thing that hardly any two people under the sun agree in
the ceremony. Some make it a sacrament, others a con-   45
venience, and others make it a jest, but among soldiers 'tis
most sacred. Our sword, you know, is our honor. That we
lay down; the hero jumps over it first and the amazon
after. Leap rogue, follow whore. The drum beats a ruff
and so to bed, that's all. The ceremony is concise.   50

BULLOCK.

And the prettiest ceremony, so full of pastime and
prodigality.

BALANCE.

What, are you a soldier?

BULLOCK.

Ay, that I am. Will your worship lend me your cane and
I'll show you how I can exercise.   55

BALANCE.

Take it. (*Strikes him over the head.*) Pray, sir, what
commission may you bear?   (*To* Silvia.)

SILVIA.

I'm called Captain, sir, by all the coffeemen, drawers,
whores, and groom porters in London, for I wear a red
coat, a sword *bien troussée*, a martial twist in my cravat, a   60
fierce knot in my periwig, a cane upon my button, piquet in
my head, and dice in my pocket.

SCALE.

Your name, pray, sir.

SILVIA.

Captain Pinch. I cock my hat with a pinch; I take snuff
with a pinch, pay my whores with a pinch. In short, I can do   65
anything at a pinch but fight and fill my belly.

60. sword *bien*] *Q1*; sword, a hat
bien *Q2-3*.

---

60. *bien troussée*] neatly arranged.
61. *piquet*] a card game played by two persons with a deck of thirty-two
cards.

BALANCE.

And pray, sir, what brought you into Shropshire?

SILVIA.

A pinch, sir. I knew that you country gentlemen want wit, and you know that we town gentlemen want money, and so—   70

BALANCE.

I understand you, sir. Here, Constable.

Enter Constable.

Take this gentleman into custody till further orders.

ROSE.

Pray, your worship, don't be uncivil to him, for he did me no hurt. He's the most harmless man in the world, for all he talks so.   75

SCALE.

Come, come, child, I'll take care of you.

SILVIA.

What, gentlemen, rob me of my freedom and my wife at once. 'Tis the first time they ever went together.

BALANCE.

Heark'e, Constable.   (*Whispers the* Constable.)

CONSTABLE.

It shall be done, sir. Come along, sir.   80

Exeunt Constable, Bullock, *and* Silvia.

BALANCE.

Come, Mr. Scale, we'll manage the spark presently.

Exeunt Balance *and* Scale.

[V.iii]   *Scene changes to* Melinda's *apartment.*
[*Enter*] Melinda *and* Worthy.

MELINDA (*aside*).

So far the prediction is right. 'Tis ten exactly. —And pray, sir, how long have you been in this traveling humor?

68. knew that you] *Q1*; knew you *Q2–3*.
79. S.D. *the* Constable] *Q1*; him *Q2–3*.

81.1. *Exeunt* ... Scale] *Q1*; *Ex. Q2–3*.
[V.iii]
0.1. *Scene* ... Melinda's] *Q1*; *Scene,* Melinda's *Q2–3*.

WORTHY.

'Tis natural, madam, for us to avoid what disturbs our
quiet.

MELINDA.

Rather the love of change, which is more natural, may be   5
the occasion of it.

WORTHY.

To be sure, madam, there must be charms in variety, else
neither you nor I should be so fond of it.

MELINDA.

You mistake, Mr. Worthy. I am not so fond of variety as to
travel for it, nor do I think it prudence in you to run your-   10
self into a certain expense and danger in hopes of precarious
pleasures which at best never answer expectation, as 'tis
evident from the example of most travelers that long more
to return to their own country than they did to go abroad.

WORTHY.

What pleasures I may receive abroad are indeed uncertain,   15
but this I am sure of, I shall meet with less cruelty among
the most barbarous nations than I have found at home.

MELINDA.

Come, sir, you and I have been jangling a great while. I
fancy if we made up our accounts we should the sooner
come to an agreement.   20

WORTHY.

Sure, madam, you won't dispute your being in my debt.
My fears, sighs, vows, promises, assiduities, anxieties,
jealousies have run on for a whole year without any
payment.

MELINDA.

A year. Oh, Mr. Worthy, what you owe to me is not to be   25
paid under a seven years' servitude. How did you use me the
year before, when taking the advantage of my innocence
and necessity, you would have made me your mistress, that
is, your slave? Remember the wicked insinuations, artful
baits, deceitful arguments, cunning pretenses? Then your   30
impudent behavior, loose expressions, familiar letters, rude
visits, remember those, those, Mr. Worthy?

10. for it] *Q1*; for't *Q2–3*.

WORTHY (*aside*).

I do remember and am sorry I made no better use of
'em. —But you may remember, madam, that—

MELINDA.

Sir, I'll remember nothing. 'Tis your interest that I should　35
forget. You have been barbarous to me; I have been cruel
to you. Put that and that together and let one balance the
other. Now if you will begin upon a new score, lay aside
your adventuring airs, and behave yourself handsomely till
Lent be over, here's my hand. I'll use you as a gentleman　40
should be.

WORTHY.

And if I don't use you as a gentlewoman should be, may
this be my poison.　　　　　　　　　　　(*Kissing her hand.*)

Enter Servant.

SERVANT.

Madam, the coach is at the door.

MELINDA.

I'm going to Mr. Balance's country house to see my cousin　45
Silvia. I have done her an injury and can't be easy till I
have asked her pardon.

WORTHY.

I dare not hope for the honor of waiting on you.

MELINDA.

My coach is full, but if you will be so gallant as to mount
your own horses and follow us, we shall be glad to be　50
overtaken. And if you bring Captain Plume with you, we
shan't have the worse reception.

WORTHY.

I'll endeavor it.　　　　　　　*Exit* Worthy *leading* Melinda.

[V.iv]　　　　　　　*The marketplace.*
　　　　　　　[*Enter*] Plume *and* Kite.

PLUME.

A baker, a tailor, a smith, and a butcher. I believe the first

45. I'm] *Q1*; I am *Q2–3*.　　　　53. S.D. Worthy] *Q1*; *om. Q2–3*.

colony planted at Virginia had not more trades in their
company than I have in mine.

KITE.

The butcher, sir, will have his hands full, for we have two
sheep stealers among us. I hear of a fellow, too, committed   5
just now for stealing of horses.

PLUME.

We'll dispose of him among the dragoons. Have we never a
poulterer among us?

KITE.

Yes, sir, the king of the gypsies is a very good one. He has
an excellent hand at a goose or a turkey. Here's Captain   10
Brazen. Sir, I must go look after the men.   *Exit* [Kite].

Enter Brazen *reading a letter.*

BRAZEN.

Um, um, um, the canonical hour. Um, um, very well. My
dear Plume, give me a buss.

PLUME.

Half a score if you will, my dear. What hast got in thy
hand, child?   15

BRAZEN.

'Tis a project for laying out a thousand pound.

PLUME.

Were it not requisite to project first how to get it in?

BRAZEN.

You can't imagine, my dear, that I want twenty thousand
pound. I have spent twenty times as much in the service.
Now, my dear, pray advise me. My head runs much upon   20
architecture. Shall I build a privateer or a playhouse?

PLUME.

An odd question. A privateer or a playhouse! 'Twill
require some consideration. Faith, I'm for a privateer.

BRAZEN.

I'm not of your opinion, my dear, for in the first place a
privateer may be ill-built.   25

PLUME.

And so may a playhouse.

2. at] *Q1*; in *Q2–3*.   7. never] *Q1*; ne'er *Q2–3*.

BRAZEN.

But a privateer may be ill-manned.

PLUME.

And so may a playhouse.

BRAZEN.

But a privateer may run upon the shallows.

PLUME.

Not so often as a playhouse.   30

BRAZEN.

But, you know, a privateer may spring a leak.

PLUME.

And I know that a playhouse may spring a great many.

BRAZEN.

But suppose the privateer come home with a rich booty;
we should never agree about our shares.

PLUME.

'Tis just so in a playhouse. So, by my advice, you shall fix   35
upon the privateer.

BRAZEN.

Agreed. But if this twenty thousand should not be in specie.

PLUME.

What twenty thousand?

BRAZEN.

Heark'e.   (*Whispers.*)

PLUME.

Married!   40

BRAZEN.

Presently. We're to meet about half a mile out of town at
the waterside. And so forth.   (*Reads.*)   "For fear I should
be known by any of Worthy's friends, you must give me
leave to wear my mask till after the ceremony, which will
make me ever yours." —Look'e there, my dear dog.   45
                    (*Shows the bottom of the letter to* Plume.)

PLUME.

Melinda. And by this light, her own hand! Once more, if
you please, my dear. Her hand exactly! Just now you say?

BRAZEN.

This minute I must be gone.

36. the] *Q1*; a *Q2–3*.   45. ever] *Q1*; forever *Q2–3*.

PLUME.

Have a little patience and I'll go with you.

BRAZEN.

No, no, I see a gentleman coming this way that may be   50
inquisitive. 'Tis Worthy; do you know him?

PLUME.

By sight only.

BRAZEN.

Have a care; the very eyes discover secrets.   *Exit* [Brazen].

Enter Worthy.

WORTHY.

To boot and saddle, Captain, you must mount.

PLUME.

Whip and spur, Worthy, or you won't mount.   55

WORTHY.

But I shall. Melinda and I are agreed. She is gone to visit
Silvia; we are to mount and follow, and could we carry a
parson with us, who knows what might be done for us
both?

PLUME.

Don't trouble your head. Melinda has secured a parson   60
already.

WORTHY.

Already! Do you know more than I?

PLUME.

Yes, I saw it under her hand. Brazen and she are to meet
half a mile hence at the waterside, there to take boat, I
suppose, to be ferried over to the Elysian fields, if there be   65
any such thing in matrimony.

WORTHY.

I parted with Melinda just now. She assured me she hated
Brazen and that she resolved to discard Lucy for daring to
write letters to him in her name.

PLUME.

Nay, nay, there's nothing of Lucy in this. I tell ye, I saw   70
Melinda's hand as surely as this is mine.

---

56. She is] *Q1*; She's *Q2–3*.   65. to the] *Q1*, *Q3*; to *Q2*.

WORTHY.

But I tell you, she's gone this minute to Justice Balance's
country house.

PLUME.

But I tell you, she's gone this minute to the waterside.

Enter a Servant.

SERVANT (*to* Worthy).

Madam Melinda has sent word that you need not trouble   75
yourself to follow her because her journey to Justice
Balance's is put off, and she's gone to take the air another
way.   [*Exit.*]

WORTHY.

How! Her journey put off?

PLUME.

That is, her journey was a put-off to you.   80

WORTHY.

'Tis plain, plain. But how, where, when is she to meet
Brazen?

PLUME.

Just now I tell you, half a mile hence at the waterside.

WORTHY.

Up or down the water?

PLUME.

That I don't know.   85

WORTHY.

I'm glad my horses are ready. Jack, get 'em out.

PLUME.

Shall I go with you?

WORTHY.

Not an inch. I shall return presently.   *Exit* [Worthy].

PLUME.

You'll find me at the hall. The justices are sitting by this
time and I must attend them.   *Exit* [Plume].   90

74.1. *a*] *Q1*; *om. Q2–3.*

[V.v]   *A Court of Justice.*
Balance, Scale, Scruple *upon the bench.* Constable, Kite, *mob* [*in attendance*]. Kite *and* Constable *advance to the front of the stage.*

KITE.

> Pray, who are those honorable gentlemen upon the bench?

CONSTABLE.

> He in the middle is Justice Balance, he on the right is Justice Scale, and he on the left is Justice Scruple, and I am Mr. Constable. Four very honest gentlemen.

KITE.

> Oh, dear sir, I'm your most obedient servant. (*Saluting*   5
> *the* Constable.) I fancy, sir, that your employment and mine are much the same, for my business is to keep people in order, and if they disobey, to knock 'em down. And then we're both staff officers.

CONSTABLE.

> Nay, I'm a sergeant myself, of the militia. Come, brother,   10
> you shall see me exercise. Suppose this a musket now.
> (*He puts his staff on his right shoulder.*)   Now I'm shouldered.

KITE.

> Ay, you're shouldered pretty well for a constable's staff,
> but for a musket you must put it on t'other shoulder, my
> dear.   15

CONSTABLE.

> Adso, that's true. Come now, give the word o'command.

KITE.

> Silence.

CONSTABLE.

> Ay, ay, so we will. We will be silent.

KITE.

> Silence, you dog, silence.
>
>   (*Strikes him over the head with his halberd.*)

0.2. Scruple] *Q1*; *and* Scruple   staff *on's right Q2–3*.
Q2–3.   12. I'm] *Q1*; I am *Q2–3*.
0.3. *to . . . stage*] *Q1*; *forward Q2–3*.   13. you're] *Q1*; you are *Q2–3*.
5. I'm] *Q1*; I am *Q2–3*.   14. t'other] *Q1*; the other *Q2–3*.
9. we're] *Q1*; We are *Q2–3*.   16. o'command] *Q1*; of command
12. S.D. *He . . . right*] *Q1*; *puts his*   *Q2–3*.

CONSTABLE.

That's the way to silence a man with a witness. What   20
d'ye mean, friend.

KITE.

Only to exercise you, sir.

CONSTABLE.

Your exercise differs so from ours that we shall ne'er agree
about it. If my own captain had given me such a rap, I had
taken the law of him.   25

Enter Plume.

BALANCE.

Captain, you're welcome.

PLUME.

Gentlemen, I thank'e.

SCRUPLE.

Come, honest Captain, sit by me. (Plume *ascends and sits
upon the bench.*) Now produce your prisoners. Here, that
fellow there, set him up. Mr. Constable, what have you to   30
say against this man?

CONSTABLE.

I have nothing to say against him, an't please ye.

BALANCE.

No? What made you bring him hither?

CONSTABLE.

I don't know, an't please your worship.

SCRUPLE.

Did not the contents of your warrant direct you what sort   35
of men to take up?

CONSTABLE.

I can't tell, an't please ye. I can't read.

SCRUPLE.

A very pretty constable truly! I find we have no business
here.

KITE.

May it please the worshipful bench, I desire to be heard in   40
this case, as being counsel for the Queen.

27. thank'e] *Q1*; thank you *Q2–3*.   32, 34, 37. an't] *Q1*; an *Q2–3*.

BALANCE.

Come, Sergeant, you shall be heard since nobody else
will speak. We won't come here for nothing.

KITE.

This man is but one man. The country may spare him and
the army wants him. Besides he's cut out by nature for a   45
grenadier: he's five foot ten inches high; he shall box,
wrestle, or dance the Cheshire Round with any man in the
county; he gets drunk every sabbath day; and he beats his
wife.

WIFE.

You lie, sirrah, you lie an't please your worship. He's the   50
best-natured, painstaking man in the parish. Witness my
five poor children.

SCRUPLE.

A wife and five children! You, Constable, you, rogue, how
durst you impress a man that has a wife and children?

SCALE.

Discharge him, discharge him.   55

BALANCE.

Hold, gentlemen. Hark'e, friend, how do you maintain
your wife and children?

PLUME.

They live upon wild fowl and venison, sir. The husband
keeps a gun and kills all the hares and partridges within
five miles round.   60

BALANCE.

A gun! Nay, if he be so good at gunning he shall have
enough on't. He may be of use against the French, for he
shoots flying to be sure.

SCRUPLE.

But his wife and children, Mr. Balance.

WIFE.

Ay, ay, that's the reason you would send him away. You   65

48. county] *Q1–2*; country *Q3*.
50. an't] *Q1*; an *Q2–3*.
51. natured, painstaking] *Q1*;
naturd'st, painstaking'st *Q2–3*.
54. children] *Q1*; five children
Q2–3.

58–60. They . . . round] Archer
gives this speech to Kite.
59. partridges] *Q1*; partridge *Q2–3*.
60. miles] *Q1*; mile *Q2–3*.

47. *Cheshire Round*] a folk dance.

know I have a child each year and you're afraid they should
come upon the parish at last.

PLUME.

Look'e there, gentlemen, the honest woman has spoke it at
once. The parish had better maintain five children this year
than six or seven the next. That fellow upon his high feeding   70
may get you two or three beggars at a birth.

WIFE.

Look'e, Mr. Captain, the parish shall get nothing by
sending him away, for I won't lose my teeming time if
there be a man left in the parish.

BALANCE.

Send that woman to the house of correction. And the man—   75

KITE.

I'll take care o' him, if you please.   (*Takes the man down.*)

SCALE.

Here, you Constable, the next. Set up that black-faced
fellow. He has a gunpowder look. What can you say
against this man, Constable?

CONSTABLE.

Nothing but that he's a very honest man.   80

PLUME.

Pray, gentlemen, let me have one honest man in my
company for the novelty's sake.

BALANCE.

What are you, friend?

MOB.

A collier; I work in the coal pits.

SCRUPLE.

Look'e, gentlemen, this fellow has a trade, and the Act of   85
Parliament here expresses that we are to impress no man
that has any visible means of a livelihood.

KITE.

May it please your worships, this man has no visible means
of a livelihood, for he works underground.

PLUME.

Well said, Kite. Besides, the army wants miners.   90

66. you're] *Q1*; you are *Q2–3*.   89. a] *Q1*; *om. Q2–3*.
76. S.D. *the man*] *Q1*; him *Q2–3*.

BALANCE.

Right. And had we an order of government for't, we could
raise you in this and the neighboring county of Stafford
five hundred colliers that would run you underground like
moles and do more service in a siege than all the miners in
the army.   95

SCRUPLE.

Well, friend, what have you to say for yourself?

MOB.

I'm married.

KITE.

Lackaday, so am I.

MOB.

Here's my wife, poor woman.

BALANCE.

Are you married, good woman?   100

WOMAN.

I'm married in conscience.

KITE.

May it please your worship, she's with child in conscience.

SCALE.

Who married you, mistress?

WOMAN.

My husband. We agreed that I should call him husband to
avoid passing for a whore, and that he should call me wife 105
to shun going for a soldier.

SCRUPLE.

A very pretty couple. Pray, Captain, will you take 'em
both.

PLUME.

What say you, Mr. Kite? Will you take care of the woman?

KITE.

Yes, sir, she shall go with us to the seaside, and there, if 110
she has a mind to drown herself, we'll take care that
nobody shall hinder her.

BALANCE.

Here, Constable, bring in my man.   *Exit* Constable.
Now, Captain, I'll fit you with a man such as you ne'er listed
in your life.   115

Enter Constable *and* Silvia.

Oh, my friend Pinch, I'm very glad to see you.

SILVIA.

Well, sir, and what then?

SCALE.

What then! Is that your respect to the bench?

SILVIA.

Sir, I don't care a farthing for you nor your bench neither.

SCRUPLE.

Look'e, gentlemen, that's enough. He's a very impudent 120
fellow, and fit for a soldier.

SCALE.

A notorious rogue, I say, and very fit for a soldier.

CONSTABLE.

A whoremaster, I say, and therefore fit to go.

BALANCE.

What think you, Captain?

PLUME.

I think he's a very pretty fellow, and therefore fit to serve. 125

SILVIA.

Me for a soldier! Send your own lazy, lubberly sons at
home, fellows that hazard their necks every day in pursuit
of a fox, yet dare not peep abroad to look an enemy in the
face.

CONSTABLE.

May it please your worships, I have a woman at the door 130
to swear a rape against this rogue.

SILVIA.

Is it your wife or daughter, booby? I ravished 'em both
yesterday.

BALANCE.

Pray, Captain, read the Articles of War. We'll see him
listed immediately.   135

(Plume *reads Articles of War against mutiny and desertion.*)

116. I'm] *Q1*; I am *Q2–3*.   127. in pursuit] *Q1*; in the pursuit
                                            Q2–3.

135.1. *Articles of War*] The Mutiny Acts and Articles of War had to be
read to a recruit before he was officially enlisted.

SILVIA.

Hold, sir. Once more, gentlemen, have a care what you do, for you shall severely smart for any violence you offer to me. And you, Mr. Balance, I speak to you particularly; you shall heartily repent it.

PLUME.

Look'e, young spark, say but one word more and I'll build 140 a horse for you as high as the ceiling, and make you ride the most tiresome journey that ever you made in your life.

SILVIA.

You have made a fine speech, good Captain Huffcap, but you had better be quiet. I shall find a way to cool your courage.   145

PLUME.

Pray, gentlemen, don't mind him; he's distracted.

SILVIA.

'Tis false. I'm descended of as good a family as any in your county. My father is as good a man as any upon your bench, and I am heir to twelve hundred pound a year.

BALANCE.

He's certainly mad. Pray, Captain, read the Articles of 150 War.

SILVIA.

Hold once more. Pray, Mr. Balance, to you I speak. Suppose I were your child, would you use me at this rate?

BALANCE.

No, faith, were you mine, I would send you to Bedlam first and into the army afterwards.   155

SILVIA.

But consider. My father, sir, he's as good, as generous, as brave, as just a man as ever served his country. I'm his only child; perhaps the loss of me may break his heart.

BALANCE.

He's a very great fool if it does. Captain, if you don't list him this minute, I'll leave the court.   160

140. spark] *Q1, Q3*; sark *Q2*.   159. it] *Q1, Q3*; he *Q2*.
147. I'm] *Q1–2*; I am *Q3*.

---

154. *Bedlam*] St. Mary of Bethlehem, a famous London hospital for the insane.

PLUME.

Kite, do you distribute the levy money to the men whilst I read.

KITE.

Ay, sir. Silence, gentlemen.

Plume reads the Articles of War.

BALANCE.

Very well. Now, Captain, let me beg the favor of you not to discharge this fellow upon any account whatsoever. Bring 165 in the rest.

CONSTABLE.

There are no more, an't please your worship.

BALANCE.

No more! There were five two hours ago.

SILVIA.

'Tis true, sir, but this rogue of a constable let the rest escape for a bribe of eleven shillings a man because he said that 170 the Act allows him but ten, so the odd shilling was clear gains.

ALL JUSTICES.

How!

SILVIA.

Gentlemen, he offered to let me get away for two guineas, but I had not so much about me. This is truth and I'm ready 175 to swear it.

KITE.

And I'll swear it; give me the book. 'Tis for the good of the service.

MOB.

May it please your worship, I gave him half a crown to say that I was an honest man, and now that your worships 180 have made me a rogue, I hope I shall have my money again.

BALANCE.

'Tis my opinion that this constable be put into the captain's hands, and if his friends don't bring four good men for his

---

161. whilst] *Q1*; while *Q2–3*. 174. get] *Q1*; go *Q2–3*.
170–171. that ... allows] *Q1*; the 180. now that] *Q1*; now since that
Act allowed *Q2–3*.   *Q2–3*.

ransom by tomorrow night, Captain, you shall carry him 185
to Flanders.

SCALE. SCRUPLE.

Agreed, agreed.

PLUME.

Mr. Kite, take the constable into custody.

KITE.

Ay, ay, sir. (*To the* Constable.) Will you please to have
your office taken from you, or will you handsomely lay 190
down your staff as your betters have done before you?

(*The* Constable *drops his staff.*)

BALANCE.

Come, gentlemen, there needs no great ceremony in
adjourning this court. Captain, you shall dine with me.

KITE.

Come, Mr. Militia Sergeant, I shall silence you now, I
believe, without your taking the law of me.   195

Exeunt omnes.

[V.vi]

Scene changes to the fields, Brazen *leading in* Lucy *masked.*

BRAZEN.

The boat is just below here.

Enter Worthy *with a case of pistols under his arm, parts* Brazen *and* Lucy.

WORTHY.

Here, sir, take your choice.   (*Offering the pistols.*)

BRAZEN.

What, pistols! Are they charged, my dear?

WORTHY.

With a brace of bullets each.

BRAZEN.

But I'm a foot officer, my dear, and never use pistols.   5
The sword is my way, and I won't be put out of my road
to please any man.

191.1. S.D. The Constable] *Q1*; 1.1. *parts . . .* Lucy] *Q1*; *om. Q2–3.*
Constable *Q2–3.*   2. S.D. *Offering the pistols*] *Q1*; *going*
[V.vi]   *between 'em and offering them pistols*
0.1. *Scene changes to the*] *Q1*; *Scene,* *Q2–3.*
the Q2–3.

–116–

WORTHY.

Nor I either, so have at you.   (*Cocks one pistol.*)

BRAZEN.

Look'e, my dear, I do not care for pistols. Pray oblige me
and let us have a bout at sharps. Dam't, there's no parrying   10
these bullets.

WORTHY.

Sir, if you han't your belly full of these, the swords shall
come in for second course.

BRAZEN.

Why then, fire and fury. I have eaten smoke from the
mouth of a cannon, sir. Don't think I fear powder, for I live   15
upon't. Let me see. (*Takes a pistol.*)   And now, sir, how
many paces distant shall we fire?

WORTHY.

Fire when you please; I'll reserve my shot till I be sure of
you.

BRAZEN.

Come, where's your cloak?   20

WORTHY.

Cloak. What d'ye mean?

BRAZEN.

To fight upon; I always fight upon a cloak. 'Tis our way
abroad.

LUCY.

Come, gentlemen, I'll end the strife.   (*Pulls off her mask.*)

WORTHY.

Lucy! Take her.   25

BRAZEN.

The devil take me if I do. Huzza!   (*Fires his pistol.*)   D'ye
hear, d'ye hear, you plaguey harridan, how those bullets
whistle. Suppose they had been lodged in my gizzard now?

LUCY.

Pray, sir, pardon me.

10. Dam't] *Q1*; damn it *Q2–3*.
16. S.D. *a pistol*] *Q1*; *one Q2–3*.
18. be] *Q1*; am *Q2–3*.

24. S.P. LUCY] Lucia *Q1*, *as in
ll. 29, 36, and 40.*
24. S.D. *Pulls off her mask*] *Q1*; *un-
masks Q2–3.*

BRAZEN.

> I can't tell, child, till I know whether my money be safe.   30
> (*Searching his pockets.*)   Yes, yes, I do pardon you, but if I
> had you in the Rose Tavern, Covent Garden, with three or
> four hearty rakes, and three or four smart napkins, I would
> tell you another story, my dear.   *Exit* [Brazen].

WORTHY.

> And was Melinda privy to this?   35

LUCY.

> No, sir. She wrote her name upon a piece of paper at the
> fortune-teller's last night, which I put in my pocket, and
> so writ above it to the captain.

WORTHY.

> And how came Melinda's journey put off?

LUCY.

> At the town's end she met Mr. Balance's steward, who   40
> told her that Mrs. Silvia was gone from her father's, and
> nobody could tell whither.

WORTHY.

> Silvia gone from her father's! This will be news to Plume.
> Go home and tell your lady how near I was being shot for
> her.   *Exeunt.*   45

[V.vii]   [Balance's *house.*]

Enter Balance *with a napkin in his hand as risen from dinner, talking with*
his Steward.

STEWARD.

> We did not miss her till the evening, sir, and then searching
> for her in the chamber that was my young master's, we
> found her clothes there, but the suit that your son left in
> the press when he went to London was gone.

BALANCE.

> The white, trimmed with silver?   5

STEWARD.

> The same.

V.vii]   Q1–3 *continue without a scene*   0.2–0.3 *talking with his*]   Q1; *and*
change.   Q2–3.

BALANCE.

You han't told that circumstance to anybody?

STEWARD.

To none but your worship.

BALANCE.

And be sure you don't. Go into the dining room and tell
Captain Plume that I beg to speak with him.   10

STEWARD.

I shall.   *Exit.*

BALANCE.

Was ever man so imposed upon? I had her promise indeed
that she should never dispose of herself without my consent.
I have consented with a witness, given her away as my act
and deed. And this, I warrant, the captain thinks will pass.   15
No, I shall never pardon him the villainy, first of robbing me
of my daughter, and then the mean opinion he must have of
me to think that I could be so wretchedly imposed upon.
Her extravagant passion might encourage her in the
attempt, but the contrivance must be his. I'll know the   20
truth presently.

Enter Plume.

Pray, Captain, what have you done with your young
gentleman soldier?

PLUME.

He's at my quarters, I suppose, with the rest of my men.

BALANCE.

Does he keep company with the common soldiers?   25

PLUME.

No, he's generally with me.

BALANCE.

He lies with you, I presume.

PLUME.

No, faith, I offered him part of my bed, but the young
rogue fell in love with Rose and has lain with her, I think,
since he came to town.   30

BALANCE.

So that between you both, Rose has been finely managed.

PLUME.

Upon my honor, sir, she had no harm from me.

BALANCE.

All's safe, I find. Now, Captain, you must know that the young fellow's impudence in court was well grounded. He said that I should heartily repent his being listed, and I do 35 from my soul.

PLUME.

Ay! For what reason?

BALANCE.

Because he is no less than what he said he was, born of as good a family as any in the county, and is heir to twelve hundred pound a year. 40

PLUME.

I'm very glad to hear it, for I wanted but a man of that quality to make my company a perfect representative of the whole commons of England.

BALANCE.

Won't you discharge him?

PLUME.

Not under a hundred pound sterling. 45

BALANCE.

You shall have it, for his father is my intimate friend.

PLUME.

Then you shall have him for nothing.

BALANCE.

Nay, sir, you shall have your price.

PLUME.

Not a penny, sir. I value an obligation to you much above a hundred pound. 50

BALANCE.

Perhaps, sir, you shan't repent your generosity. Will you please to write his discharge in my pocket book. (*Gives his book.*) In the meantime, we'll send for the gentleman. Who waits there?

Enter Servant.

Go to the captain's lodgings and inquire for Mr. Wilful. Tell 55 him his captain wants him here immediately.

35. that] *Q1*; *om. Q2–3.*
35. I do] *Q1*; so I do *Q2–3.*
39. is] *Q1–2*; he is *Q3.*

45. a] *Q1*; an *Q2–3.*
49. a] *Q1*; an *Q2–3.*
55. lodgings] *Q1*; lodging *Q2–3.*

–120–

SERVANT.

Sir, the gentleman's below at the door inquiring for the captain.

PLUME.

Bid him come up. Here's the discharge, sir.

BALANCE.

Sir, I thank you.   (*Aside.*)   'Tis plain he had no hand in't.   60

Enter Silvia.

SILVIA.

I think, Captain, you might have used me better than to leave me yonder among your swearing, drunken crew. And you, Mr. Justice, might have been so civil as to have invited me to dinner, for I have eaten with as good a man as your worship.   65

PLUME.

Sir, you must charge our want of respect upon our ignorance of your quality. But now you're at liberty. I have discharged you.

SILVIA.

Discharged me!

BALANCE.

Yes, sir, and you must once more go home to your father.   70

SILVIA.

My father. Then I'm discovered! Oh, sir, I expect no pardon.   (*Kneeling.*)

BALANCE.

Pardon. No, no, child, your crime shall be your punishment. Here, Captain, I deliver her over to the conjugal power for her chastisement. Since she will be a wife, be you   75
a husband, a very husband. When she tells you of her love, upbraid her with her folly. Be modishly ungrateful because she has been unfashionably kind. And use her worse than you would anybody else, because you can't use her so well as she deserves.   80

PLUME.

And are you Silvia in good earnest?

67. you're] *Q1*; you are *Q2–3*.   71. I'm] *Q1*; I am *Q2–3*.

SILVIA.

Earnest. I have gone too far to make it a jest, sir.

PLUME.

And do you give her to me in good earnest?

BALANCE.

If you please to take her, sir.

PLUME.

Why then, I have saved my legs and arms and lost my   85
liberty; secure from wounds I'm prepared for the gout.
Farewell subsistence and welcome taxes. Sir, my liberty
and hopes of being a general are much dearer to me than
your twelve hundred pound a year, but to your love,
madam, I resign my freedom, and to your beauty, my   90
ambition, greater in obeying at your feet than commanding
at the head of an army.

Enter Worthy.

WORTHY.

I'm sorry to hear, Mr. Balance, that your daughter is lost.

BALANCE.

So am not I, sir, since an honest gentleman has found her.

Enter Melinda.

MELINDA.

Pray, Mr. Balance, what's become of my cousin Silvia?   95

BALANCE.

Your cousin Silvia is talking yonder with your cousin
Plume.

MELINDA. WORTHY.

How!

SILVIA.

Do you think it strange, cousin, that a woman should
change? But, I hope, you'll excuse a change that has pro-   100
ceeded from constancy. I altered my outside because I was
the same within, and only laid by the woman to make sure
of my man. That's my history.

MELINDA.

Your history is a little romantic, cousin, but since success

84. S.P. BALANCE] *Q1*; *Q2-3 give*   86. I'm] *Q1*; I am *Q2-3*.
the speech to Silvia.   93. I'm] *Q1*; I am *Q2-3*.

has crowned your adventures, you will have the world o' 105
your side, and I shall be willing to go with the tide, provided
you pardon an injury I offered you in the letter to your
father.

PLUME.

That injury, madam, was done to me, and the reparation
I expect shall be made to my friend. Make Mr. Worthy 110
happy, and I shall be satisfied.

MELINDA.

A good example, sir, will go a great way. When my cousin
is pleased to surrender, 'tis probable I shan't hold out much
longer.

Enter Brazen.

BRAZEN.

Gentlemen, I am yours. Madam, I am not yours.   115

MELINDA.

I'm glad on't, sir.

BRAZEN.

So am I. You have got a pretty house here, Mr. Laconic.

BALANCE.

'Tis time to right all mistakes. My name, sir, is Balance.

BRAZEN.

Balance. Sir, I'm your most obedient. I know your whole
generation. Had not you an uncle that was governor of the 120
Leeward Islands some years ago?

BALANCE.

Did you know him?

BRAZEN.

Intimately, sir. He played at billiards to a miracle. You had
a brother, too, that was captain of a fireship. Poor Dick, he
had the most engaging way with him of making punch, and 125
then his cabin was so neat. But his boy Jack was the most
comical bastard, ha, ha, ha, a pickled dog. I shall never
forget him.

PLUME.

Well, Captain, are you fixed in your project yet? Are you
still for the privateer?   130

107. you] *Q1*; you'll *Q2–3*.   127. ha, ha, ha] *Q1*; ha, ha *Q2–3*.
119. I'm] *Q1*; I am *Q2–3*.

BRAZEN.

> No, no, I had enough of a privateer just now. I had like to
> have been picked up by a cruiser under false colors, and a
> French picaroon for ought I know.

PLUME.

> But have you got your recruits, my dear?

BRAZEN.

> Not a stick, my dear.   135

PLUME.

> Probably I shall furnish you.

Enter Rose *and* Bullock.

ROSE.

> Captain, Captain, I have got loose once more and have
> persuaded my sweetheart Cartwheel to go with us, but you
> must promise not to part with me again.

SILVIA.

> I find Mrs. Rose has not been pleased with her bedfellow.   140

ROSE.

> Bedfellow! I don't know whether I had a bedfellow or not.

SILVIA.

> Don't be in a passion, child. I was as little pleased with
> your company as you could be with mine.

BULLOCK.

> Pray, sir, dunna be offended at my sister. She's something
> underbred. But if you please, I'll lie with you in her stead. 145

PLUME.

> I have promised, madam, to provide for this girl. Now
> will you be pleased to let her wait upon you, or shall I take
> care of her?

SILVIA.

> She shall be my charge, sir. You may find it business enough
> to take care of me.   150

BULLOCK.

> Ay, and of me, Captain, for wauns, if ever you lift your
> hand against me, I'll desert.

PLUME.

> Captain Brazen shall take care o'that. My dear, instead of
> the twenty thousand pound you talked of, you shall have the
> twenty brave recruits that I have raised, at the rate they 155

cost me. My commission I lay down to be taken up by some
braver fellow that has more merit and less good fortune,
while I endeavor by the example of this worthy gentleman
to serve my Queen and country at home.

> With some regret I quit the active field,   160
> Where glory full reward for life does yield;
> But the recruiting trade with all its train,
> Of lasting plague, fatigue, and endless pain,
> I gladly quit, with my fair spouse to stay,
> And raise recruits the matrimonial way.   165

163. lasting] *Q1*; endless *Q2–3*.

Appendix A

Variant Passages

[II.i] ll. 51–58

PLUME.

    You are indebted to me a welcome, madam, since the hopes
of receiving it from this fair hand was the principal cause
of my seeing England.

SILVIA.

    I have often heard that soldiers were sincere. Shall I venture
to believe public report?   5

PLUME.

    You may when 'tis backed by private insurance, for I
swear, madam, by the honor of my profession, that what-
ever dangers I went upon, it was with the hope of making
myself more worthy of your esteem, and if I ever had
thoughts of preserving my life, 'twas for the pleasure of   10
dying at your feet.

SILVIA.

    Well, well, you shall die at my feet or where you will, but
you know, sir, there is a certain will and testament to be
made beforehand.

[IV.i] ll. 57–68

SILVIA.

    I would qualify myself for the service.

PLUME.

    Hast thou really a mind to the service?

SILVIA.

    Yes, sir, so let her go.

ROSE.

    Pray, gentlemen, don't be so violent.

PLUME.

Come, leave it to the girl's own choice. Will you belong to   5
me or to that gentleman?

ROSE.

Let me consider; you're both very handsome.

PLUME.

Now the natural inconstancy of her sex begins to work.

ROSE.

Pray, sir, what will you give me?

BULLOCK.

Don't be angry, sir, that my sister should be mercenary,   10
for she's but young.

SILVIA.

Give thee, child. I'll set thee above scandal. You shall have
a coach with six before and six behind, an equipage to make
vice fashionable and put virtue out of countenance.

PLUME.

Pho, that's easily done. I'll do more for thee, child. I'll buy   15
you a furbelow scarf and give you a ticket to see a play.

BULLOCK.

A play! Wauns, Rose, take the ticket and let's see the show.

SILVIA.

Look'e, Captain, if you won't resign, I'll go list with Captain
Brazen this minute.

PLUME.

Will you list with me if I give up my title?   20

SILVIA.

I will.

PLUME.

Take her.

Appendix B

Chronology

Approximate years are indicated by *.

Political and Literary Events   *Life and Major Works of Farquhar*

1631
John Dryden born.

1633
Samuel Pepys born.

1635
Sir George Etherege born.*

1640
Aphra Behn born.

1641
William Wycherley born.*

1642
First Civil War began (ended 1646).
Theaters closed by Parliament.
Thomas Shadwell born.*

1648
Second Civil War.

1649.
Execution of Charles I.

1650
Jeremy Collier born.

1651
Hobbes' *Leviathan* published.

1652
First Dutch War began (ended
1654).
Thomas Otway born.

1653
Nathaniel Lee born.*

1656
D'Avenant's *THE SIEGE OF
RHODES* performed at Rutland
House.

1657
John Dennis born.
1658
Death of Oliver Cromwell.
D'Avenant's *THE CRUELTY OF THE SPANIARDS IN PERU* performed at the Cockpit.
1660
Restoration of Charles II.
Theatrical patents granted to Thomas Killigrew and Sir William D'Avenant, authorizing them to form, respectively, the King's and the Duke of York's Companies.
Pepys began his diary.
1661
Cowley's *THE CUTTER OF COLEMAN STREET.*
1662
Charter granted to the Royal Society.
1663
Dryden's *THE WILD GALLANT.*
Tuke's *THE ADVENTURES OF FIVE HOURS.*
1664
Sir John Vanbrugh born.
Dryden's *THE RIVAL LADIES.*
Dryden and Howard's *THE INDIAN QUEEN.*
Etherege's *THE COMICAL REVENGE.*
1665
Second Dutch War began (ended 1667).
Great Plague.
Dryden's *THE INDIAN EMPEROR.*
Orrery's *MUSTAPHA.*
1666
Fire of London.
Death of James Shirley.
1667
Milton's *Paradise Lost* published.
Sprat's *The History of the Royal Society* published.
Dryden's *SECRET LOVE.*

1668
Death of D'Avenant.
Dryden made Poet Laureate.
Dryden's *An Essay of Dramatic Poesy* published.
Shadwell's *THE SULLEN LOVERS*.

1669
Pepys terminated his diary.
Susannah Centlivre born.

1670
William Congreve born.
Dryden's *THE CONQUEST OF GRANADA*, Part I.

1671
Dorset Garden Theatre (Duke's Company) opened.
Colley Cibber born.
Milton's *Paradise Regained* and *Samson Agonistes* published.
Dryden's *THE CONQUEST OF GRANADA*, Part II.
THE REHEARSAL, by the Duke of Buckingham and others.
Wycherley's *LOVE IN A WOOD*.

1672
Third Dutch War began (ended 1674).
Joseph Addison born.
Richard Steele born.
Dryden's *MARRIAGE À LA MODE*.

1674
New Drury Lane Theatre (King's Company) opened.
Death of Milton.
Nicholas Rowe born.
Thomas Rymer's *Reflections on Aristotle's Treatise of Poesy* (translation of Rapin) published.

1675
Dryden's *AURENG-ZEBE*.
Wycherley's *THE COUNTRY WIFE.**

1676
Etherege's *THE MAN OF MODE*.
Otway's *DON CARLOS*.

Shadwell's *THE VIRTUOSO*.
Wycherley's *THE PLAIN DEALER*.

1677
Dryden's *ALL FOR LOVE*.
Lee's *THE RIVAL QUEENS*.
Rymer's *Tragedies of the Last Age Considered* published.

George Farquhar born.*

1678
Popish Plot.
Bunyan's *Pilgrim's Progress* (Part I) published.

1679
Exclusion Bill introduced.
Death of Thomas Hobbes.
Death of Roger Boyle, Earl of Orrery.
Charles Johnson born.

1680
Death of Samuel Butler.
Death of John Wilmot, Earl of Rochester.
Dryden's *THE SPANISH FRIAR*.
Lee's *LUCIUS JUNIUS BRUTUS*.
Otway's *THE ORPHAN*.

1681
Charles II dissolved Parliament at Oxford.
Dryden's *Absalom and Achitophel* published.
Tate's adaptation of *KING LEAR*.

1682
The King's and the Duke of York's Companies merged into the United Company.
Dryden's *The Medal, MacFlecknoe*, and *Religio Laici* published.
Otway's *VENICE PRESERVED*.

1683
Rye House Plot.
Death of Thomas Killigrew.

1685
Death of Charles II; accession of James II.
Revocation of the Edict of Nantes.
The Duke of Monmouth's Rebellion.

Death of Otway.
John Gay born.
Crowne's *SIR COURTLY NICE*.
Dryden's *ALBION AND AL-BANIUS*.

1687
Death of the Duke of Buckingham.
Dryden's *The Hind and the Panther*
published.
Newton's *Principia* published.

1688
The Revolution.
Alexander Pope born.
Shadwell's *THE SQUIRE OF ALSATIA*.

1689
The War of the League of Augsburg
began.
Toleration Act.
Death of Aphra Behn.
Shadwell made Poet Laureate.
Dryden's *DON SEBASTIAN*.
Shadwell's *BURY FAIR*.

1690
Battle of the Boyne.
Locke's *Two Treatises of Government*
and *An Essay Concerning Human
Understanding* published.

1691
Death of Etherege.
Langbaine's *An Account of the English
Dramatic Poets* published.

1692
Death of Lee.
Death of Shadwell.
Tate made Poet Laureate.

1693
George Lillo born.
Rymer's *A Short View of Tragedy*
published.
Congreve's *THE OLD BACHE-LOR*.

1694
Death of Queen Mary.　　　　　　　　Entered Trinity College, Dublin.
Southerne's *THE FATAL MAR-RIAGE*.

1695
Group of actors led by Thomas Betterton leave Drury Lane and establish a new company at Lincoln's Inn Fields.
Congreve's *LOVE FOR LOVE*.
Southerne's *OROONOKO*.

1696
Cibber's *LOVE'S LAST SHIFT*.
Vanbrugh's *THE RELAPSE*.

1697
Treaty of Ryswick ended the War of the League of Augsburg.
Charles Macklin born.
Congreve's *THE MOURNING BRIDE*.
Vanbrugh's *THE PROVOKED WIFE*.

Went to London.

1698
Collier controversy started with the publication of *A Short View of the Immorality and Profaneness of the English Stage*.

1699

LOVE AND A BOTTLE produced at Drury Lane in mid-December.
The Adventures of Covent Garden (anecdotal narrative) published December 15.

THE CONSTANT COUPLE, OR A TRIP TO THE JUBILEE produced at Drury Lane in late November.

1700
Death of Dryden.
Blackmore's *Satire Against Wit* published.
Congreve's *THE WAY OF THE WORLD*.

1701
Act of Settlement.
War of the Spanish Succession began.
Death of James II.
Rowe's *TAMERLANE*.
Steele's *THE FUNERAL*.

SIR HARRY WILDAIR produced at Drury Lane in April.
Love and Business (collection of prose and verse) published.

1702
Death of William III; accession of Anne.
The Daily Courant began publication.

THE INCONSTANT (adapted from Fletcher's *THE WILD GOOSE CHASE*) produced at Drury Lane in early March.

APPENDIX B

Cibber's *SHE WOULD AND SHE WOULD NOT*.

THE TWIN RIVALS opened at Drury Lane on December 14.

1703
Death of Samuel Pepys.
Rowe's *THE FAIR PENITENT*.

Married to Margaret Pemell.

1704
Capture of Gibraltar; Battle of Blenheim.
Defoe's *The Review* began publication (1704–1713).
Swift's *A Tale of a Tub* and *The Battle of the Books* published.
Cibber's *THE CARELESS HUSBAND*.

Commissioned Lieutenant of Grenadiers.
THE STAGE-COACH (comic afterpiece) produced at Lincoln's Inn Fields in January.

1705
Haymarket Theatre opened.
Steele's *THE TENDER HUSBAND*.

Sent on recruiting duty to Lichfield and then to Shrewsbury.

1706
Battle of Ramillies.

THE RECRUITING OFFICER opened at Drury Lane on April 8.

1707
Union of Scotland and England.
Henry Fielding born.

Died in a London garret on April 29.
THE BEAUX' STRATAGEM opened at the Haymarket on March 8.
Love's Catechism (largely a patchwork of passages from *THE BEAUX' STRATAGEM*) published.
Barcelona (poem) published.*

1708
Downes' *Roscius Anglicanus* published.

1709
Samuel Johnson born.
Rowe's edition of Shakespeare published.
The Tatler began publication (1709–1710).
Centlivre's *THE BUSY BODY*.

1711
Shaftesbury's *Characteristics* published.
The Spectator began publication (1711–1712).

–134–

Pope's *An Essay on Criticism* published.

1713
Treaty of Utrecht ended the War of the Spanish Succession.
Addison's *CATO*.

1714
Death of Anne; accession of George I.
Steele became Governor of Drury Lane.
John Rich assumed management of Lincoln's Inn Fields.
Centlivre's *THE WONDER: A WOMAN KEEPS A SECRET*.
Rowe's *JANE SHORE*.

1715
Jacobite Rebellion.
Death of Tate.
Rowe made Poet Laureate.
Death of Wycherley.

1716
Addison's *THE DRUMMER*.

1717
David Garrick born.
Cibber's *THE NON-JUROR*.
Gay, Pope, and Arbuthnot's *THREE HOURS AFTER MARRIAGE*.

1718
Death of Rowe.
Centlivre's *A BOLD STROKE FOR A WIFE*.

1719
Death of Addison.
Defoe's *Robinson Crusoe* published.
Young's *BUSIRIS, KING OF EGYPT*.

1720
South Sea Bubble.
Samuel Foote born.
Steele suspended from the Governorship of Drury Lane (restored 1721).
Steele's *The Theatre* (periodical) published.
Hughes' *THE SIEGE OF DAMASCUS*.

1721
Walpole became first Minister.

1722
Steele's *THE CONSCIOUS LOVERS.*

1723
Death of Susannah Centlivre.
Death of D'Urfey.

1725
Pope's edition of Shakespeare published.

1726
Death of Jeremy Collier.
Death of Vanbrugh.
Law's *Unlawfulness of Stage Entertainments* published.
Swift's *Gulliver's Travels* published.

1727
Death of George I; accession of George II.
Death of Sir Isaac Newton.
Arthur Murphy born.

1728
Pope's *Dunciad* published.
Cibber's *THE PROVOKED HUSBAND* (expansion of Vanbrugh's fragment *A JOURNEY TO LONDON*).
Gay's *THE BEGGAR'S OPERA.*

1729
Goodman's Fields Theatre opened.
Death of Congreve.
Death of Steele.
Edmund Burke born.

1730
Cibber made Poet Laureate.
Oliver Goldsmith born.
Thomson's *The Seasons* published.
Fielding's *THE AUTHOR'S FARCE*; *TOM THUMB* (revised as *THE TRAGEDY OF TRAGEDIES*, 1731).

1731
Death of Defoe.
Lillo's *THE LONDON MERCHANT.*

1732
Covent Garden Theatre opened.
Death of Gay.
George Colman the elder born.
Fielding's *THE COVENT GAR-DEN TRAGEDY*; *THE MODERN HUSBAND*.
Charles Johnson's *CAELIA*.

1733
Pope's *An Essay on Man* (Epistles I–III) published (Epistle IV, 1734).

1734
Death of Dennis.
The Prompter began publication (1734–1736).
Theobald's edition of Shakespeare published.
Fielding's *DON QUIXOTE IN ENGLAND*.

1736
Fielding led the "Great Mogul's Company of Comedians" at the Little Theatre in the Haymarket (1736–1737).
Fielding's *PASQUIN*.
Lillo's *THE FATAL CURIOSITY*.

1737
The Stage Licensing Act.
Dodsley's *THE KING AND THE MILLER OF MANSFIELD*.
Fielding's *THE HISTORICAL REGISTER FOR 1736*.